INDIRA GANDHI

WORLD LEADERS PAST & PRESENT

INDIRA GANDHI

Francelia Butler

1986
CHELSEA HOUSE PUBLISHERS
NEW YORK
NEW HAVEN PHILADELPHIA

The author dedicates this book to her granddaughter, Charlotte Megan Wandell, and gratefully acknowledges the invaluable help of Pratima and Ram Raj Upadhyay, Kamla Srinivasan, and Jean Hankins.

Printed and bound in the United States of America.

Frontispiece courtesy of UPI/Bettmann Newsphotos

First Printing

Library of Congress Cataloging in Publication Data

Butler, Francelia. INDIRA GANDHI

(World leaders past & present)
Bibliography: p.
Includes index.
1. Gandhi, Indira, 1917–1984. 2. Prime ministers—India—Biography. I. Title. II. Series.
DS481.G23B88 1986 954.04'5'0924 [B] [92] 86—4138

ISBN 0-87754-596-0

Chelsea House Publishers

133 Christopher Street, New York, NY 10014

345 Whitney Avenue, New Haven, CT 06510

5014 West Chester Pike, Edgemont, PA 19028

Contents

CHELSEA HOUSE PUBLISHERS

WORLD LEADERS PAST & PRESENT

ADENAUER
ALEXANDER THE GREAT
MARK ANTONY
KING ARTHUR
KEMAL ATATÜRK
CLEMENT ATTLEE
BEGIN
BEN-GURION
BISMARCK
LEON BLUM
BOLÍVAR
CESARE BORGIA
BRANDT
BREZHNEV
CAESAR
CALVIN
CASTRO
CATHERINE THE GREAT
CHARLEMAGNE
CHIANG KAI-SHEK
CHURCHILL
CLEMENCEAU
CLEOPATRA
CORTÉS
CROMWELL
DANTON
DE GAULLE
DE VALERA
DISRAELI
EISENHOWER
ELEANOR OF AQUITAINE
QUEEN ELIZABETH I
FERDINAND AND ISABELLA
FRANCO
FREDERICK THE GREAT
INDIRA GANDHI
GANDHI
GARIBALDI
GENGHIS KHAN
GLADSTONE
HAMMARSKJÖLD
HENRY VIII
HENRY OF NAVARRE
HINDENBURG
HITLER
HO CHI MINH
KING HUSSEIN
IVAN THE TERRIBLE
ANDREW JACKSON
JEFFERSON
JOAN OF ARC
POPE JOHN XXIII
LYNDON JOHNSON
BENITO JUÁREZ
JFK
KENYATTA
KHOMEINI
KHRUSHCHEV
MARTIN LUTHER KING, JR.
KISSINGER
LENIN
LINCOLN
LLOYD GEORGE
LOUIS XIV
LUTHER
JUDAS MACCABEUS
MAO
MARY, QUEEN OF SCOTS
GOLDA MEIR
METTERNICH
MUSSOLINI
NAPOLEON
NASSER
NEHRU
NERO
NICHOLAS II
NIXON
NKRUMAH
PERICLES
PERÓN
QADDAFI
ROBESPIERRE
ELEANOR ROOSEVELT
FDR
THEODORE ROOSEVELT
SADAT
STALIN
SUN YAT-SEN
TAMERLAINE
THATCHER
TITO
TROTSKY
TRUDEAU
TRUMAN
QUEEN VICTORIA
WASHINGTON
CHAIM WEIZMANN
WOODROW WILSON
XERXES
ZHOU ENLAI

ON LEADERSHIP

Arthur M. Schlesinger, jr.

LEADERSHIP, it may be said, is really what makes the world go round. Love no doubt smooths the passage; but love is a private transaction between consenting adults. Leadership is a public transaction with history. The idea of leadership affirms the capacity of individuals to move, inspire and mobilize masses of people so that they act together in pursuit of an end. Sometimes leadership serves good purposes, sometimes bad; but whether the end is benign or evil, great leaders are those men and women who leave their personal stamp on history.

Now, the very concept of leadership implies the proposition that individuals can make a difference. This proposition has never been universally accepted. From classical times to the present day, eminent thinkers have regarded individuals as no more than the agents and pawns of larger forces, whether the gods and goddesses of the ancient world or, in the modern era, race, class, nation, the dialectic, the will of the people, the spirit of the times, history itself. Against such forces, the individual dwindles into insignificance.

So contends the thesis of historical determinism. Tolstoy's great novel *War and Peace* offers a famous statement of the case. Why, Tolstoy asked, did millions of men in the Napoleonic wars, denying their human feelings and their common sense, move back and forth across Europe slaughtering their fellows? "The war," Tolstoy answered, "was bound to happen simply because it was bound to happen." All prior history predetermined it. As for leaders, they, Tolstoy said, "are but the labels that serve to give a name to an end and, like labels, they have the least possible connection with the event." The greater the leader, "the more conspicuous the inevitability and the predestination of every act he commits." The leader, said Tolstoy, is "the slave of history."

Determinism takes many forms. Marxism is the determinism of class, Nazism the determinism of race. But the idea of men and women as the slaves of history runs athwart the deepest human instincts. Rigid determinism abolishes the idea of human freedom—the assumption of free choice that underlies every move we make, every word we speak, every thought we think. It abolishes the idea of human responsibility, since it is manifestly unfair to reward or punish people for actions that are by definition beyond their control. No one can live consistently by any deterministic creed. The Marxist states prove this themselves by their extreme susceptibility to the cult of leadership.

More than that, history refutes the idea that individuals make no difference. In December 1931 a British politician crossing Park Avenue in New York City between 76th and 77th Streets around ten-thirty at night looked in the wrong direction and was knocked down by an automobile—a moment, he later recalled, of a man aghast, a world aglare: "I do not understand why I was not broken like an eggshell or squashed like a gooseberry." Fourteen months later an American politician, sitting in an open car in Miami, Florida, was fired on by an assassin; the man beside him was hit. Those who believe that individuals make no difference to history might well ponder whether the next two decades would have been the same had Mario Contasini's car killed Winston Churchill in 1931 and Giuseppe Zangara's bullet killed Franklin Roosevelt in 1933. Suppose, in addition, that Adolf Hitler had been killed in the street fighting during the Munich *Putsch* of 1923 and that Lenin had died of typhus during the First World War. What would the 20th century be like now?

For better or for worse, individuals do make a difference. "The notion that a people can run itself and its affairs anonymously," wrote the philosopher William James, "is now well known to be the silliest of absurdities. Mankind does nothing save through initiatives on the part of inventors, great or small, and imitation by the rest of us—these are the sole factors in human progress. Individuals of genius show the way, and set the patterns, which common people then adopt and follow."

Leadership, James suggests, means leadership in thought as well as in action. In the long run, leaders in thought may well make the greater difference to the world. But, as Woodrow Wilson once said, "Those only are leaders of men, in the general eye, who lead in action. . . . It is at their hands that new thought gets its translation into the crude language of deeds." Leaders in thought often invent in solitude and obscurity, leaving to later generations the tasks of imitation. Leaders in action—the leaders portrayed in this series—have to be effective in their own time.

And they cannot be effective by themselves. They must act in response to the rhythms of their age. Their genius must be adapted, in a phrase of William James's, "to the receptivities of the moment." Leaders are useless without followers. "There goes the mob," said the French politician hearing a clamor in the streets. "I am their leader. I must follow them." Great leaders turn the inchoate emotions of the mob to purposes of their own. They seize on the opportunities of their time, the hopes, fears, frustrations, crises, potentialities.

They succeed when events have prepared the way for them, when the community is waiting to be aroused, when they can provide the clarifying and organizing ideas. Leadership ignites the circuit between the individual and the mass and thereby alters history.

It may alter history for better or for worse. Leaders have been responsible for the most extravagant follies and most monstrous crimes that have beset suffering humanity. They have also been vital in such gains as humanity has made in individual freedom, religious and racial tolerance, social justice and respect for human rights.

There is no sure way to tell in advance who is going to lead for good and who for evil. But a glance at the gallery of men and women in *World Leaders—Past and Present* suggests some useful tests.

One test is this: do leaders lead by force or by persuasion? By command or by consent? Through most of history leadership was exercised by the divine right of authority. The duty of followers was to defer and to obey. "Theirs not to reason why,/ Theirs but to do and die." On occasion, as with the so-called "enlightened despots" of the 18th century in Europe, absolutist leadership was animated by humane purposes. More often, absolutism nourished the passion for domination, land, gold and conquest and resulted in tyranny.

The great revolution of modern times has been the revolution of equality. The idea that all people should be equal in their legal condition has undermined the old structures of authority, hierarchy and deference. The revolution of equality has had two contrary effects on the nature of leadership. For equality, as Alexis de Tocqueville pointed out in his great study *Democracy in America*, might mean equality in servitude as well as equality in freedom.

"I know of only two methods of establishing equality in the political world," Tocqueville wrote. "Rights must be given to every citizen, or none at all to anyone . . . save one, who is the master of all." There was no middle ground "between the sovereignty of all and the absolute power of one man." In his astonishing prediction of 20th-century totalitarian dictatorship, Tocqueville explained how the revolution of equality could lead to the "*Führerprinzip*" and more terrible absolutism than the world had ever known.

But when rights are given to every citizen and the sovereignty of all is established, the problem of leadership takes a new form, becomes more exacting than ever before. It is easy to issue commands and enforce them by the rope and the stake, the concentration camp and the *gulag*. It is much harder to use argument and achievement to overcome opposition and win consent. The Founding Fathers of the United States understood the difficulty. They believed that history had given them the opportunity to decide, as

Alexander Hamilton wrote in the first Federalist Paper, whether men are indeed capable of basing government on "reflection and choice, or whether they are forever destined to depend . . . on accident and force."

Government by reflection and choice called for a new style of leadership and a new quality of followership. It required leaders to be responsive to popular concerns, and it required followers to be active and informed participants in the process. Democracy does not eliminate emotion from politics; sometimes it fosters demagoguery; but it is confident that, as the greatest of democratic leaders put it, you cannot fool all of the people all of the time. It measures leadership by results and retires those who overreach or falter or fail.

It is true that in the long run despots are measured by results too. But they can postpone the day of judgment, sometimes indefinitely, and in the meantime they can do infinite harm. It is also true that democracy is no guarantee of virtue and intelligence in government, for the voice of the people is not necessarily the voice of God. But democracy, by assuring the rights of opposition, offers built-in resistance to the evils inherent in absolutism. As the theologian Reinhold Niebuhr summed it up, "Man's capacity for justice makes democracy possible, but man's inclination to injustice makes democracy necessary."

A second test for leadership is the end for which power is sought. When leaders have as their goal the supremacy of a master race or the promotion of totalitarian revolution or the acquisition and exploitation of colonies or the protection of greed and privilege or the preservation of personal power, it is likely that their leadership will do little to advance the cause of humanity. When their goal is the abolition of slavery, the liberation of women, the enlargement of opportunity for the poor and powerless, the extension of equal rights to racial minorities, the defense of the freedoms of expression and opposition, it is likely that their leadership will increase the sum of human liberty and welfare.

Leaders have done great harm to the world. They have also conferred great benefits. You will find both sorts in this series. Even "good" leaders must be regarded with a certain wariness. Leaders are not demigods; they put on their trousers one leg after another just like ordinary mortals. No leader is infallible, and every leader needs to be reminded of this at regular intervals. Irreverence irritates leaders but is their salvation. Unquestioning submission corrupts leaders and demeans followers. Making a cult of a leader is always a mistake. Fortunately hero worship generates its own antidote. "Every hero," said Emerson, "becomes a bore at last."

The signal benefit the great leaders confer is to embolden the rest of us to live according to our own best selves, to be active, insistent, and resolute in affirming our own sense of things. For great leaders attest to the reality of human freedom against the supposed inevitabilities of history. And they attest to the wisdom and power that may lie within the most unlikely of us, which is why Abraham Lincoln remains the supreme example of great leadership. A great leader, said Emerson, exhibits new possibilities to all humanity. "We feed on genius. . . . Great men exist that there may be greater men."

Great leaders, in short, justify themselves by emancipating and empowering their followers. So humanity struggles to master its destiny, remembering with Alexis de Tocqueville: "It is true that around every man a fatal circle is traced beyond which he cannot pass; but within the wide verge of that circle he is powerful and free; as it is with man, so with communities."

—New York

1

India in Transition

> ***Let us be strong, tolerant, and disciplined, for tolerance and discipline are the very foundations of democracy.***
> —INDIRA GANDHI

On December 31, 1965, Prime Minister Lal Bahadur Shastri of India arrived in the central Asian city of Tashkent to sign a peace treaty with Field Marshal Ayub Khan, the ruler of Pakistan. The short but vicious war that had been fought earlier that year between India and Pakistan had ended in a resounding victory for India, and Shastri's cool and clear-headed leadership had made him immensely popular. In fact, just two weeks before he left for Tashkent, Shastri had attracted an audience of 1 million people to a Bombay political rally, a remarkable display of popular enthusiasm for an Indian national leader. Many people had begun to believe that the traditional turbulence of Indian politics might soon become less pronounced — that the world's most populous democracy might unite behind the tough little man who the Pakistanis had dismissed as a mere "bird wrestler" prior to their ill-fated invasion.

Eleven days after Shastri's departure, India's new mood of optimism was shattered. On January 10, 1966, word was flashed from Tashkent to Delhi, India's capital, that Shastri had died of a heart at-

Indira Gandhi (1917–84), one of the most controversial national leaders of modern times, served as prime minister of India from 1966 to 1977 and from 1980 to 1984. In governing her poverty-stricken and overpopulated country, she displayed both a passion for democracy and a strong tendency toward authoritarianism.

THE BETTMANN ARCHIVE

AP/WIDE WORLD

Two-year-old Indira poses with her parents, Jawaharlal Nehru (1889–1934) and Kamala Kaul (1899–1936).

tack. Suddenly, India was thrown into turmoil. Who would succeed Shastri as leader of the country's ruling party, the Indian National Congress, and thus, as prime minister? Would it be veteran politician Morarji Desai, the proud and influential head of the Ministry of Finance? Or would it be his popular but less experienced counterpart at the Ministry of Information and Broadcasting, Indira Gandhi? Gandhi was the daughter of India's most revered statesman, Jawaharlal Nehru, who had been instrumental in winning Indian independence from Great Britain in 1947.

As the election for the Congress party leadership approached, Desai moved quickly to secure the office he had wanted ever since Nehru's death in 1964. But his many enemies within the party, determined to block his election at any cost, threw their weight behind the 48-year-old Indira Gandhi. Their support, along with Indira's personal popularity as Nehru's daughter, was enough to swing the election in her favor. She won by a landslide — 355 votes to Desai's 169 — and on January 19, 1966, Indira Gandhi became India's first woman prime minister.

Only 50 years earlier, the idea that their prime minister could be an Indian — especially an Indian *woman* — would have been inconceivable to most Indians. A century or two before that, a united India would have seemed equally improbable. When European travelers first visited the Indian subcontinent in the 11th century it was splintered into small, frequently warring kingdoms. Its ethnic, geographic, and religious diversity had defeated all attempts at unification.

> ***If a woman has the qualifications and ability for any profession, she should be in it.***
> —INDIRA GANDHI

India was a land of great natural wealth: European explorers returning from the distant "Indies" brought back not only exciting tales but exotic spices, such as pepper, ginger, and cinnamon. Indian spices were soon in great demand in the courts and palaces of Europe, but there was no easy way for merchants to reach India: the land route through the deserts of Persia was long and treacherous, and the sea route, around the southern tip of Africa, meant a voyage of many months.

In 1608 merchants of the East India Company, a

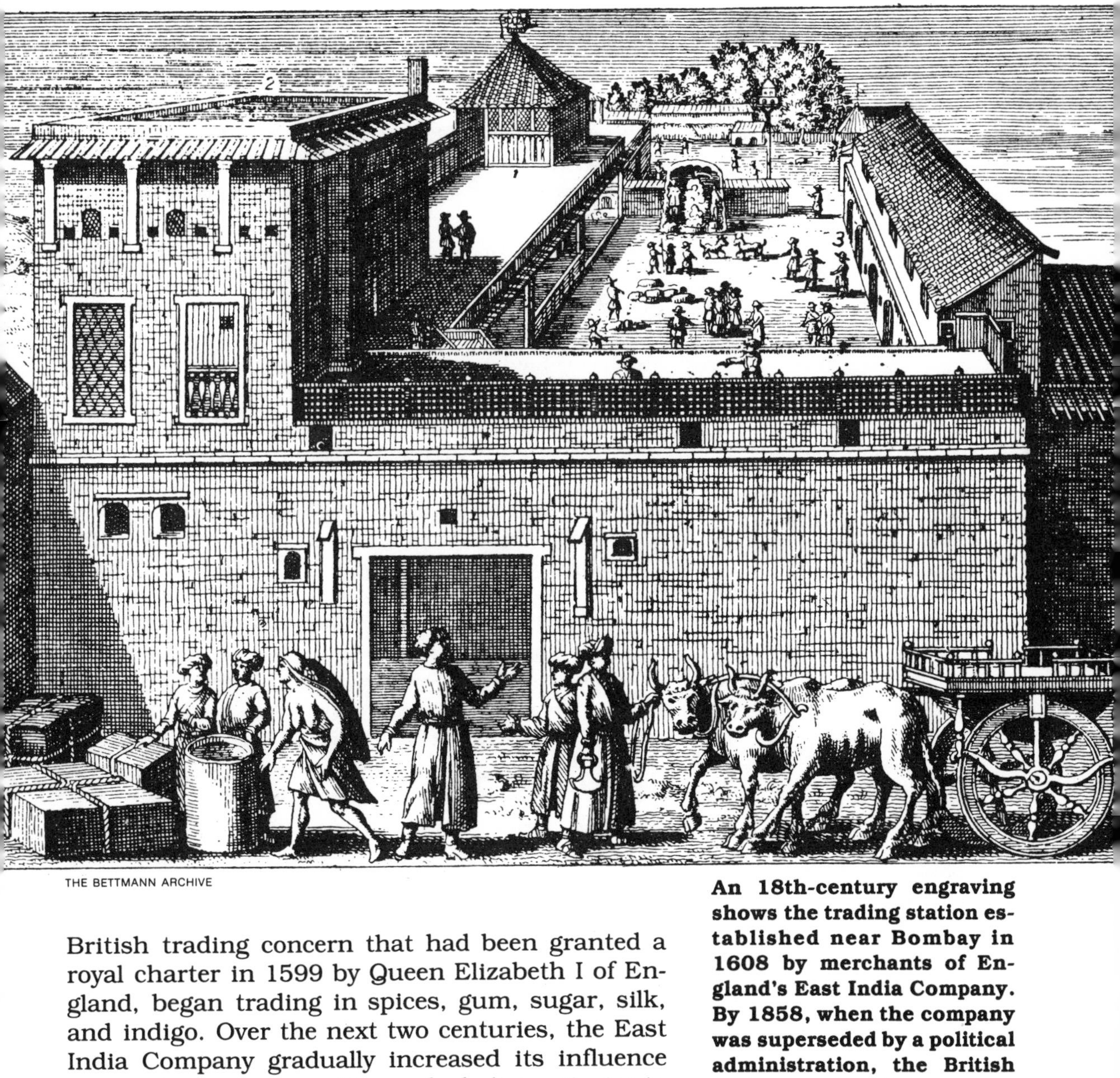

THE BETTMANN ARCHIVE

An 18th-century engraving shows the trading station established near Bombay in 1608 by merchants of England's East India Company. By 1858, when the company was superseded by a political administration, the British had gained political, economic, and military supremacy in much of India.

British trading concern that had been granted a royal charter in 1599 by Queen Elizabeth I of England, began trading in spices, gum, sugar, silk, and indigo. Over the next two centuries, the East India Company gradually increased its influence over India, annexing cities and whole territories to ensure a continued supply of raw materials.

By the end of the 18th century, the British had imposed their own laws and customs on the Indian territories under their control. The East India Company built railways and established British-style courts and schools, as well as a civil service and military system. The British also outlawed Indian customs they considered barbaric, including *suttee* (the burning of widows along with their deceased husbands), the murder of infant girls (who were often considered useless in Indian society), and the bloodthirsty cult of the goddess *Kali*. Most of all, the British gave India's many different peoples a common language: English.

Gradually, many social reforms were made and the number of English-speaking, British-educated natives grew, but many Indians resented the fact that they were still second-class citizens in their own country; they could not vote, hold public meetings, or publish newspapers critical of the British. Although many Indians served in the army of the East India Company or in the Indian Civil Service, senior positions in those institutions were always reserved for British officers and administrators. While some Indians prospered under the East India Company, many of the British who settled in India became wealthy beyond their wildest dreams, surrounding themselves with Indian servants and living in luxury.

I believe in the doctrine of nonviolence as a weapon of the weak. I believe in the doctrine of nonviolence as a weapon of the strongest. I believe that a man is the strongest soldier for daring to die unarmed.

—MOHANDAS GANDHI

In 1857 Indian soldiers in the army of the East India Company struck the first real blow for independence: a bloody rebellion that was quickly put down by the British. In the wake of the Indian Mutiny — as the revolt came to be known — the British government dissolved the East India Company and assumed direct responsibility for the administration of India. For the first time in its history, India was now united under a single ruler — the British viceroy, who ruled on behalf of the British monarch.

The Nehru family had come to Delhi, the historical capital of India, in the early 18th century, and had taken their family name from the *nehar*, or canal, that flowed by their home. After the Indian Mutiny British soldiers took savage reprisals against the residents of Delhi and many other cities in India, looting and murdering indiscriminately. To escape the violence, the Nehrus moved to Agra, and later made their home in the northern city of Allahabad, at the confluence of the Jumna and Ganges rivers. In Allahabad, the British and Indian communities coexisted in peace. The Nehru family prospered, and by the end of the 19th century, Motilal Nehru — Indira's grandfather — was in many ways more British than Indian. A wealthy lawyer, he spoke perfect English, wore Western-style suits, and played tennis with both his British and Indian friends. His family sat down to dinner around a table set with elegant china and silverware, and only occasionally crouched on mats for a traditional Indian meal. Even his house, *Anand Bhavan* ("House of Joy"),

Rebel cavalrymen of the East India Company's Bengal army attack British troops during the Indian Mutiny (1857–58). Although the conflict ended in a British victory, it also caused the downfall of the East India Company, which was blamed by the British government for ignoring the signs of unrest that had preceded the rebellion.

THE BETTMANN ARCHIVE

> **Satyagraha . . . *means "holding on to truth," hence "truth-force." I have also called it "love-force" or "soul-force." I discovered in the earliest stages that pursuit of truth did not admit of violence being inflicted on one's opponent, but that he must be weaned from error by patience and sympathy.***
>
> —MOHANDAS GANDHI

was like a European palace. Anand Bhavan boasted a dozen bedrooms, expensive tapestries, an indoor swimming pool, tennis courts, croquet lawns, and a fleet of foreign cars. Motilal made sure that his only son, Jawaharlal, who was born in 1889, received the best education that Britain could offer. The young man attended Harrow (an extremely prestigious prep school), Cambridge University, and London's Inner Temple law school.

Motilal, like many Indians who had benefited from a British education and who greatly enjoyed living in the Western manner, felt torn between the two cultures. On the surface, he was very much the polished Englishman, but he knew he would always be an Indian at heart, with his roots in a culture thousands of years older than England's. Jawaharlal felt this inner conflict even more deeply, since he had been educated in England and had adopted the ideas and attitudes of an upper-class Englishman. Following his return to India, Jawaharlal began to find that his true loyalty was to his homeland. It was at this time that events combined to propel Jawaharlal toward a career in politics.

In 1916 the young lawyer attended the opening ceremonies of the Hindu University, in the eastern city of Benares, and heard for the first time the words of a man who would have a profound effect on the future of India: Mohandas Karamchand Gandhi. A frail, mild-mannered man sporting wire-rimmed spectacles and a homespun *dhoti*, or long peasant's loincloth, Gandhi commenced his speech by apologizing for talking in English and then launched into an impassioned plea for self-government for India. His largely upper-class audience, which was composed of high-ranking British officials and numerous Indian princes and princesses, listened in dismay as Gandhi exhorted educated Indians to serve the subcontinent's poor, who, he claimed, were the true base of India's political power.

The same year, Jawaharlal married Kamala Kaul, the wife chosen for him by his father. On November 19, 1917, Kamala gave birth to a daughter. When the baby was brought in to be shown to her grand-

AP/WIDE WORLD

Indira's father, Jawaharlal, is seated on the floor between his own father, Motilal (1861–1931), and his mother, Swaruprani (1872–1938). The portrait, which includes other family members and a British governess (right), was made about 1910 at the Nehru family's home in Allahabad.

parents, Motilal's wife, Swaruprani, expressed disappointment. As far as Swaruprani was concerned, having another girl in the family would simply mean another dowry to pay. (Since women were traditionally looked upon as burdens in India, a dowry, or "bride price," was offered by a young woman's family to the family of the man who married her and "took her off their hands.") But Motilal angrily silenced his wife. "Have we made any distinction between our son and our daughters?" he asked her. "Do you not love them equally? This daughter of Jawaharlal, for all you know, may prove better than a thousand sons." Motilal then announced that the new baby would be named Indira, after his mother.

2

Mohandas Gandhi

I can say without the slightest hesitation, and yet in all humility, that those who say that religion has nothing to do with politics do not know what religion means.
—MOHANDAS GANDHI

Mohandas Gandhi, the man who had so inspired Jawaharlal shortly before the birth of his daughter, was one of the most important political figures of the 20th century. In India, he was known as the *Mahatma*, or "great soul," for his kindness and compassion; British statesman Winston Churchill, however, called Gandhi a "seditious . . . lawyer . . . posing as a fakir" (a *fakir* is an Indian holy man), and spoke of the "nauseating and humiliating" spectacle of Gandhi "striding half-naked up the steps of the viceregal palace . . . to parley on equal terms with the representative of the King-Emperor." This man, so admired by some and so hated by others, never held public office. His political power came solely from the love and devotion of hundreds of millions of Indians.

Gandhi was born in Porbandar, a small city-state in western India, on October 2, 1869. He was the youngest child of an administrator at the court of the prince of Porbandar. Because he was painfully shy, the young Gandhi made few friends, and spent much of his time reading. His father, Karamchand, was proud of his "intellectual" son, and hoped that

THE BETTMANN ARCHIVE

Gandhi in 1910, when he was working as a lawyer in South Africa. Gandhi's search for a response to the South African government's discriminatory policies toward Indian immigrants led him to develop the principle of *satyagraha* ("soul force"), or nonviolent resistance.

Indira and leading Indian nationalist Mohandas K. Gandhi (1869–1948) in 1941. Gandhi, who understood that his country's millions of poor constituted the only base of effective political power in India, transformed the Indian National Congress from a middle-class debating society into a formidable mass movement during the 1920s and 1930s.

AP/WIDE WORLD

Untouchables—members of the lowest Hindu *caste*, or social order, sweep a village street in present-day India. The nation has technically been a secular state since 1950, but the caste system—of which Nehru and Gandhi strongly disapproved—remains firmly in place.

UPI/BETTMANN NEWSPHOTOS

he would follow in his footsteps. Karamchand Gandhi died when Mohandas was 17. The following year, Karamchand's older brother offered to send the young man to England to study law. After promising his mother that he would not touch wine, women, or meat (the Gandhis were vegetarians), Mohandas left for England in September 1888. There, he studied law at London's Inner Temple, just as Jawaharlal Nehru was to do some 20 years later.

When Gandhi returned to India in 1891, his shyness and inexperience as a lawyer made it difficult for him to find work. Finally, a local company asked him to be their representative in Pretoria, South Africa; he quickly agreed. His ship docked in the British-ruled eastern province of Natal, South Africa, in May 1893. At that time, the 400,000 blacks and 51,000 Indians (originally brought to South Africa as laborers) in Natal were governed by a few thousand whites of Dutch and British descent. Although the Indians had prospered as merchants and craftsmen, they were still treated as second-class citizens, made to live in their own communities, and segregated both by the laws and the prejudices of the ruling whites.

Gandhi was introduced to South African racism on the train to Pretoria; an Englishman asked the conductor to have Gandhi removed from the first-class coach because he was "colored." When Gandhi protested, he was thrown off the train at the next station. This experience affected him deeply, and, after a number of similar incidents, he began to consider working to organize the Indian community. In 1894 Gandhi founded the Natal Indian Congress, which monitored events in South Africa as they related to the Indians there. When his contract with his employers expired, he decided to remain in South Africa in order to lead the Indian community in its struggle against segregation and discrimination.

Demonstrating the exalted status given to them by Hinduism (the religion practiced by the majority of Indians), sacred cows wander the streets of Delhi. Gandhi and Nehru disagreed about whether or not religion and politics were compatible. Gandhi insisted that they were; Nehru considered religion a barrier to political progress.

UPI/BETTMANN NEWSPHOTOS

Gandhi and his employees sit in front of his Johannesburg, South Africa, law office in 1913. At right is Sonja Schlesin, a stenographer who applied for employment with Gandhi because she admired his ideals. Gandhi, in turn, greatly admired Sonja, whom he called "the jewel of my house."

On several occasions, Gandhi was attacked and pelted with stones by angry white mobs, but he steadfastly refused to meet violence with violence. Gandhi felt that even the most sweeping social reforms could be accomplished peacefully, through what he called *satyagraha* (soul force). *Satyagraha* came to mean an organized campaign of civil disobedience against the authorities. "In *satyagraha*," Gandhi wrote, "physical force is forbidden." Instead, Gandhi's followers simply refused to obey laws that they felt were unjust or to cooperate in any way with the South African authorities. In this manner, Gandhi believed, they would "conquer their adversaries" with patience and sympathy instead of with violence.

Gandhi led the battle against segregation in South Africa for two years. In 1915 he returned to India, ready to put *satyagraha* to work against the British government there. He began by founding an *ashram*, a community made up of his followers, near Ahmedabad in western India, and he immediately caused an uproar by inviting "untouchables" to join the community. (Hinduism, India's predominant religion, divides society into *castes*, or social levels. At the top are the *Brahmans*, or members of the priestly class; at the bottom of this system are the *untouchables*. These people, believed by Hindus to be atoning for sins committed in an earlier life, are given the dirtiest and most demeaning jobs, and are not permitted to touch other Hindus, or even to touch objects that other Hindus might touch. As a boy, Gandhi had ignored his mother's warnings and shared his candy with an untouchable boy who cleaned the Gandhi family's toilets.)

By February 1916, when Gandhi spoke at the opening of the Hindu University before an audience that included the young Jawaharlal Nehru as well as the British viceroy, the movement for Indian independence was more than just a dream. The time was right in India for the emergence of a national leader, a man who could show India the path to freedom from the British. That man was to be Mohandas Gandhi.

UPI/BETTMANN NEWSPHOTOS

Gandhi and his wife Kasturbai (1869–1944) in 1921. The Indian leader confused the British as often as he enraged them. In 1921 the British viceroy, Viscount Erleigh (1860–1935), wrote: "[Gandhi's] religious and moral views are admirable . . . but I confess that I find it difficult to understand his practice of them in politics."

3
A Political Childhood

My first memory was of burning foreign cloth and imported articles in the courtyard of the house: the whole family did it.
—INDIRA GANDHI

The setting of Indira's childhood was peaceful and idyllic — green parrots and the scent of lemon trees filled the air as she played in the gardens of Anand Bhavan. Events in India at that time, however, were neither peaceful nor idyllic, as the young Indira soon discovered.

Both Indira's father, Jawaharlal, and her grandfather, Motilal, were members of the Indian National Congress, a political body founded in 1885 by an Englishman named Allan Hume, who was sympathetic toward the rising nationalism of the Indian middle class. Motilal, who believed that the British would eventually return India to the Indians, favored peaceful cooperation with the British government. Jawaharlal, however, became increasingly radical on the subject of Indian independence, and supported Gandhi's call for a campaign of civil disobedience against the British. Gandhi and his many followers were willing to go to jail or even to die for the cause of a free India. They were equally prepared to face jail or death rather than use violence against their opponents. This was a radically new idea, not only to the Indians but also to the British.

THE BETTMANN ARCHIVE

An Indian servant waits on a British woman in Lucknow, India, in the early 1920s. Most British administrators in India viewed the people they ruled as somehow inferior to themselves. Their prejudices were shared by their monarch, King George V (1865–1936), who once wrote of "the utter lack of courage, moral and political, among the natives."

Indira and Jawaharlal in London in 1938. Touring Europe that year, Jawaharlal became further convinced of the European colonial powers' moral cowardice when the British and French governments abandoned their ally, Czechoslovakia, to a takeover by fascist Germany.

UPI/BETTMANN NEWSPHOTOS

Motilal was horrified by the notion of civil disobedience. How could he, a lawyer and an upper-class Brahman, stoop to breaking the law? Jawaharlal argued frequently with Motilal, who secretly feared that his son would be jailed for treason by the British government.

> ***She is like a little flower which bends in the wind . . . but I think she will not break.***
>
> —FRAU TOLLER
> family friend, describing young Indira

In 1919, responding to new legislation that gave the British increased powers of repression, Gandhi called for a general strike. In Amritsar, a large city in the northern Punjab state, thousands of men and women gathered in Jallianwalla Bagh park for a peaceful (although illegal) demonstration. Infuriated, a British army officer, Brigadier General Reginald Dyer, ordered his troops to seal off the exit to the park and then to fire into the crowd. The unarmed Indians had nowhere to run; within minutes, 379 were killed and at least 1,200 wounded. The terrible massacre at Jallianwalla Bagh park shocked all India. The British, instead of reprimanding Dyer, continued with the crackdown and imposed martial law throughout the Punjab.

As a member of the commission appointed by the Congress to investigate the massacre, Jawaharlal traveled to Amritsar, where he was shocked by what he saw. "I realized then, more vividly than I had ever done before," he later wrote, "how brutal and immoral imperialism was and how it had eaten into the souls of the British upper classes." On the train home to Allahabad, Jawaharlal was dismayed to hear a group of British officers bragging about the slaughter and became even more horrified when he discovered that the loudest member of the group was none other than General Dyer.

In December 1919 Motilal was elected president of the Congress, and he and Jawaharlal and Gandhi soon became known as the "Congress Trinity" — the father, the son, and the holy ghost. Together, they worked tirelessly to promote the cause of Indian independence. "I became wholly absorbed in the movement," wrote Jawaharlal. "I almost forgot my family, my wife, my daughter."

When the findings of the British report on the Jallianwalla Bagh incident were published in April 1920, it was discovered that the investigative committee had divided along racial lines. However, it was not just the Indians on the committee who recommended that Dyer be censured. Some English committee members also condemned him. Shortly after the report was published, Britain's House of Lords (the upper house of its Parliament) registered its approval of Dyer, and many upper-class Britons contributed to a fund in appreciation of his services. Shocked, Gandhi declared that "cooperation in any shape or form with this satanic government is sinful." In August 1920 he persuaded the Congress to approve and organize a campaign of noncooperation with the government.

Nationalist feeling in India continued to grow. Thousands of Indians began to follow Gandhi's example by dressing in Indian homespun cloth and refusing to wear garments imported from England or made from British fabrics. Even the Nehrus discarded their European clothing. They built a bonfire on their lawn to burn their London-made suits and costly European draperies. When the four-year-old Indira was reminded that *she* had a foreign treasure — her favorite doll — she bravely made the sacrifice and tossed the doll into the flames. Although she felt ill for several days afterward — "I felt as if I was murdering someone," she wrote later — Indira had made her own small contribution to the fight for independence.

When her father told her the story of Joan of Arc, the French nationalist leader who was burned at the stake by the British in 1431, Indira imagined that she was Joan of Arc. Standing on the porch with her arms raised, she told her aunt, "Someday I am going to lead my people to freedom as Joan of Arc did."

In November 1921 the Prince of Wales — the heir to the British throne — arrived in India for an official visit. Gandhi called for a boycott of the government-organized celebrations. Much to the annoyance of the British, most Indians supported the boycott. The British immediately cracked down on the Congress: both Motilal and Jawaharlal were arrested and sentenced to six-month prison terms.

In the Nehru household, these were the first of

THE BETTMANN ARCHIVE

The governor of Madras presents a banner to the commanding officer of an Indian army battalion in 1925. There were two major military forces in India throughout the colonial period— British regular troops and the Indian army, which was recruited in India and led by British officers.

THE BETTMANN ARCHIVE

Responding to Gandhi's call for a boycott of all British goods—including textiles—Indian women work at their spinning wheels in 1920. Gandhi's insistence that his followers use only Indian-made goods directly affected the young Indira: she bravely threw her foreign-made doll into the bonfire that her parents had made of their imported clothing and draperies.

many arrests that disrupted family life and resulted in what Indira later called "an extremely insecure childhood." Her father was in and out of prison, and, with increasing frequency, so was her grandfather. Even her mother, Kamala, an enthusiastic supporter of Gandhi, spent time in jail. Since the Nehrus refused to acknowledge the authority of British laws, policemen would come to their house and seize valuables to pay for fines. Little Indira would scream at the policemen and try to protect her family's property. Once, she almost chopped off a policeman's thumb with a knife. Indian politics were so much a part of Indira's childhood that she would even pretend to be a political activist, climbing up on a table and making impassioned speeches about Gandhi and independence to a captive audience of servants.

Indira's schooling also became a political issue in the Nehru family. At first she was sent to the Modern School in Allahabad, an Indian public school. But Motilal decided she would get a better education at a private school, and selected St. Cecilia's. Her father, who was in jail at the time, protested that St. Cecilia's, since it was run by British women, should also be made a target of the noncooperation campaign. Furthermore, said Jawaharlal, he did not want his daughter to become a "little Miss Muffet" like some of the young women he had met in England. As a result, Indira attended neither school; she was taught by private tutors instead. Indira, an only child who was often cared for by relatives while her parents were in jail or speaking at political rallies, was now cut off from the companionship of other children as well.

In 1926 Indira's mother contracted tuberculosis and, on the advice of her doctors, traveled to Switzerland for treatment. Jawaharlal and Indira went with her, and Indira was enrolled in the International School in Geneva and then in L'Ecole Nouvelle in Bex. There she studied French and music, learned how to ski, and, for almost the first time in her life, enjoyed the company of both parents at the same time. For once, Indira was happy.

UPI/BETTMANN NEWSPHOTOS

Armed Indian policemen disperse a crowd of nationalist demonstrators in Bombay in 1932. The protesters were calling for the release of Gandhi, who had been arrested, along with Nehru and other Congress party leaders, for demanding a renewed campaign of civil disobedience.

4

The Monkey Brigade

> ***You were a child of a turbulent world.***
> —JAWAHARLAL NEHRU
> in a letter to Indira

Back in India in 1927, Indira attended St. Mary's Convent School in Allahabad. Motilal finished his term as president of the Congress in 1929, and Jawaharlal was chosen to succeed him. In his inauguration address, Jawaharlal called for complete independence for India, but, unlike Gandhi, he was willing to achieve independence by any means: "If this Congress, or the nation at any future time, comes to the conclusion that methods of violence will rid us of slavery, then I have no doubt that I will adopt them. Violence is bad, but slavery is far worse."

Indira, who was now 12 years old, wanted desperately to join the Congress party, but there was one small problem — members had to be at least 18. Indira's political upbringing, however, had made her rebellious, so instead of just sitting at home while her parents made speeches and went to jail for the cause of Indian independence, she decided to organize her own version of the Congress. She called it the *Vanar Sena*, or "Monkey Brigade," after a character called the Monkey General in an Indian folktale.

AP/WIDE WORLD

By the time India gained its independence in 1947, British statesman Winston Churchill (1874–1965) had been an outspoken opponent of Indian nationalism for more than four decades. When Indira later met Churchill, she said, "We never hated you personally." The aging imperialist, completely baffled, replied, "But I did, I did!"

Indira in 1955, the year in which she was appointed to the Congress Working Committee, the highest authority within the Congress party. Following her appointment, Indira became involved in the activities of the Congress party's women's department, which enabled her to give political expression to the feminism she had learned from her mother.

AP/WIDE WORLD

Indian nationalists gather salt from a Bombay beach in the wake of the 1930 Salt March. Gandhi had staged the protest to demonstrate his opposition to the British monopoly on salt production in India and to symbolize his rejection of British authority.

UPI/BETTMANN NEWSPHOTOS

> *There are so many sides to her which were never allowed to grow: so many springs inside her which were never allowed to flow, because of her peculiar circumstances.*
>
> —MRS. JAYAKAR
> family friend, describing
> Indira's adolescence

Over 1,000 children from all walks of life attended the first meeting of the Monkey Brigade. Indira's parents, who were at first amused by the idea of a children's organization within the independence movement, soon realized how useful the "Monkeys" could be. The Monkey Brigade quickly took over all sorts of tasks from the Congress: cooking and serving food, making flags and bandages for demonstrations, stuffing and addressing envelopes. Especially during confrontations with the British authorities, a Monkey could do things that an adult could not — as Indira said, "Sometimes a house might be surrounded by police and you could not send out a message. But nobody bothered about an urchin hopping in and out through the police cordon."

As the Monkey Brigade grew, so did Gandhi's campaign of civil disobedience. At that time, the British had a monopoly on the production and marketing of salt in India; Indians were forbidden to make their own salt or buy it from anyone other than British merchants. On March 12, 1930, in a dramatic and symbolic gesture to protest the British salt laws, the 61-year-old Gandhi and 78 of his followers left their home province of Gujarat and set off by foot for the seacoast village of Dandi, some 200 miles away. By the time the marchers reached Dandi, thousands of Indians had joined their protest. On April 6 Gandhi walked down to the seashore and, in defiance of British law, picked up a handful of salt from the beach. Inspired by Gandhi's gesture, people all over India began to ignore the law and gather salt themselves.

The British responded with thousands of arrests and a series of bloody confrontations. In Bombay, Indian policemen attacked a group of protesters and beat them severely; over 300 were injured, and at least two died. In Peshawar, on the Afghanistan border, the police used machine guns against the demonstrators. Jawaharlal was arrested in April, Gandhi in May, and Motilal in June. Shortly before he was arrested, Motilal had donated his mansion, Anand Bhavan, to the Congress, renaming it *Swaraj Bhavan*, or "Independence House." The palatial mansion was converted into a hospital for Indians injured during demonstrations; the Monkey Brigade helped take care of the patients. Meanwhile, the Nehrus — those who were not in jail — moved into a smaller house on the property.

Throughout the summer of 1930, Lord Irwin, the British viceroy, negotiated with the imprisoned Gandhi through Indian intermediaries. Motilal was released in September because his health was de-

Motilal Nehru (right) joins his son Jawaharal in prison in June 1930. The 69-year-old Motilal's physical condition deteriorated rapidly within weeks of his admission to prison, and the British authorities released him on medical grounds in September of that same year. The veteran nationalist's health had been ruined, however; he died on February 5, 1931.

UPI/BETTMANN NEWSPHOTOS

teriorating rapidly and it had become apparent that he did not have long to live. Jawaharlal was released on October 14, 1930, and was then arrested yet again two weeks later for defying an order forbidding him to speak in public.

From prison, Jawaharlal wrote letter after letter to his daughter, describing the history of the world as he saw it — "a large family of nations" — and touching on many other issues. Indira later wrote that her father's letters "helped to form my mind in a way that no other education did, because they helped me to see things in perspective . . . I never saw an Indian problem merely as an Indian problem, but as an international one."

In January 1931 Gandhi and many detained Congress leaders, including Jawaharlal, were set free. Jawaharlal rushed home to see his father, who died on February 5.

In August 1931 Gandhi traveled to London to represent the Congress at the Round Table conference which the British government had convened to consider constitutional reforms for India. While some Englishmen, like Churchill, loathed Gandhi and bristled at the very notion of a free India, others admired his courage and considered Indian inde-

An Indian fakir, or holy man, sits on a bed of nails to demonstrate his imperviousness to pain. In 1931 Churchill called Gandhi "a seditious lawyer . . . now posing as a fakir of a type well known in the East."

THE BETTMANN ARCHIVE

THE BETTMANN ARCHIVE

A cheering crowd greets Gandhi in London in 1931. Visiting England to confer with government officials about India's colonial status, Gandhi was received cordially by King George V, and enthusiastically by the public, which seemed largely sympathetic to his quest for India's freedom.

pendence inevitable. An English textile worker who heard Gandhi speak in Lancashire said, "I am one of the unemployed because of Gandhi's campaign against British textiles, but if I was in India, I would say the same thing that Mr. Gandhi is saying." Gandhi's visit to England also helped to focus world attention on India's plight: Gandhi became an international symbol for civil rights and independence from colonial rule.

5

Growing Up

She was fascinated by stories about Joan of Arc.
—KRISHNA NEHRU HUTHEESING
Indira's aunt

For the Nehrus 1931 was not a good year. Jawaharlal was shocked and saddened by his father's death, and the civil disobedience campaign had been suspended while Gandhi was in London negotiating with the British government. Kamala was sick again with tuberculosis and had to be hospitalized in Bombay. Nehru knew that he might be arrested again at any time, so he decided to send Indira to a boarding school in Poona, almost 1,000 miles away.

Indira devoted most of her time to her studies, but she also liked to go hiking and climbing in the hills surrounding Poona. She had the lead role in a school dance production, and when her classmates held a mock parliament, she was elected prime minister. Perhaps the high point of her years in Poona came in 1932, when she visited Gandhi at the nearby Yeravada Prison.

The negotiations in London the previous year had come to nothing, and when Gandhi returned to India, the British government had once again imprisoned him. At the same time, the government announced new voting regulations that called for

UPI/BETTMANN NEWSPHOTOS

Gandhi bows to his followers shortly after his release from prison in January 1931. The following February, he met with the viceroy of India, Lord Irwin (1881–1959), who persuaded him to represent the Congress party at the London Round Table Conference on independence for India.

Indira speaks at a farmers' convention in 1978. Although Indira often spoke positively about socialism, her left-wing critics accused her of praising the system only to maintain the political allegiance of the working class.

UPI/BETTMANN NEWSPHOTOS

separate elections for the untouchables. Gandhi had always believed that the segregation of the untouchables was morally wrong — no better, in fact, than the South African treatment of blacks and Indians. He also believed that separating the votes of high-caste Hindus and untouchables would weaken the Indian nationalist cause. He resolved to go on a hunger strike, a "fast unto death," until Hindus and untouchables made a political alliance, and conditions for the untouchables improved dramatically. Gandhi fasted for seven days, and the results were indeed dramatic: although the political chasm between Hindus and untouchables remained wide, temples all over the country opened their doors to untouchables, and in many villages, untouchables were allowed to use wells and roads for the first time. In Allahabad, Indira's grandmother Swaruprani (who was widely known as a conservative Hindu) accepted food from an untouchable.

THE BETTMANN ARCHIVE

Gandhi (at right of large chair) attends the Round Table Conference in September 1931. Although Gandhi's appearance at the conference was a major concession to the British, the viceroy still refused to allow the Congress Working Committee—which he had declared illegal in 1930—to resume its activities.

When Indira visited Gandhi in prison, she told him how her classmates in Poona had supported his efforts. The students had all fasted for 24 hours, and had gone into the city to care for untouchable children. Indira herself had adopted an untouchable girl as her "little sister." Gandhi later told Jawaharlal how healthy and happy Indira looked, now that she had a cause to fight for.

After graduating from Poona in 1933, Indira rejoined her parents. Later that year, Jawaharlal and Kamala decided that Indira should continue her education at Santiniketan, in Bengal, where the internationally famous philosopher and poet Rabindranath Tagore had established an academy. At Santiniketan, which was as much a community as a college, teachers and students lived and worked together. Under Tagore, who became a major influence upon her, Indira studied classical Indian dance. "Her teachers, all in one voice, praise her,"

Tagore wrote to Indira's father, "and I know she is extremely popular with the students."

Kamala's health continued to deteriorate, and Indira had to leave Santiniketan after only 20 months to accompany her mother back to Europe for treatment. There, the doctors told Kamala that she would probably not recover. The British released Jawaharlal from prison in September 1935 so that he could join his wife and daughter in Bavaria. In January of the following year, the Nehrus moved to Lausanne, Switzerland, to enable Kamala to live out her last days with the best possible medical care. While in Europe, Jawaharlal received word that he had been reelected president of the Congress, and he made plans to return to India. On February 28, 1936, Kamala died.

Rabindranath Tagore (1861–1941), the internationally famous poet, painter, and educator who established the academy at Santiniketan where Indira studied from 1934 to 1935. Indira greatly enjoyed life at Tagore's academy; she later wrote that the time she spent there had contained "moments of joy, memories to cherish."

AP/WIDE WORLD

UPI/BETTMANN NEWSPHOTOS

An untouchable woman draws water from a well belonging to a high-caste Hindu. Gandhi's 1932 fast helped to improve the social position of the untouchables, the Hindu community's lowliest members.

"Many people know that part which was played by my father and my grandfather," Indira wrote later, "but in my opinion, a more important part was played by my mother." Kamala had encouraged Jawaharlal to defy his father and follow Gandhi in the early days, and had stood by his side throughout the struggle for independence. And in a land where women had always been subservient to men, Kamala was an ardent feminist: according to her husband, she had been "a champion of woman's rights against the tyranny of man."

Indira's childhood had never been easy, but with Kamala's death, for better or worse, her childhood was over.

6

Love and War

I feel she requires a course of field or factory work to bring her down from the clouds. She will have to come down and if she does not do so early, she will do so late, and then the process will be painful.

—JAWAHARLAL NEHRU
reflecting on Indira's
character during adolescence

After Kamala's death, Nehru returned to India to preside over the Congress, and Indira went on to England, where she hoped to attend Oxford University. Because her schooling had been interrupted so many times by her father's political activities and her mother's poor health, Indira failed the entrance examination. Instead of going to Oxford, she enrolled at Badminton, an exclusive preparatory school near Bristol, a seaport on the west coast of England.

A classmate of Indira's at Badminton, novelist Iris Murdoch, had this to say about her: "She was extraordinarily beautiful, but looked very frail. At times, it was almost as if she would be carried away by the wind. She was a very dignified and aloof girl, but it was obvious to all of us that she was very unhappy and couldn't wait to get back to her country. . . . We knew that Indira had just lost her mother and that her father was being permanently locked up by the British in India. As a result everyone looked after her and even spoilt her, but it didn't work. She wanted to go back."

Indira finally passed the Oxford entrance exami-

AP/WIDE WORLD

Economist and politician Feroze Gandhi (1913–60) trains for a cricket match in 1953. Indira's 1942 decision to marry Feroze, who was not a Hindu, angered many of her coreligionists and forced Nehru himself to defend the union. "I fail to see the relevance of all this [controversy]," he wrote. "One marries an individual, not a community."

Indira talks with Virginia Rusk, wife of U.S. Secretary of State Dean Rusk (b. 1909), at a 1961 Washington, D.C., banquet honoring Nehru. The numerous official visits on which Indira accompanied her father gave her a familiarity with international affairs that was to be extremely useful in her later career.

UPI/BETTMANN NEWSPHOTOS

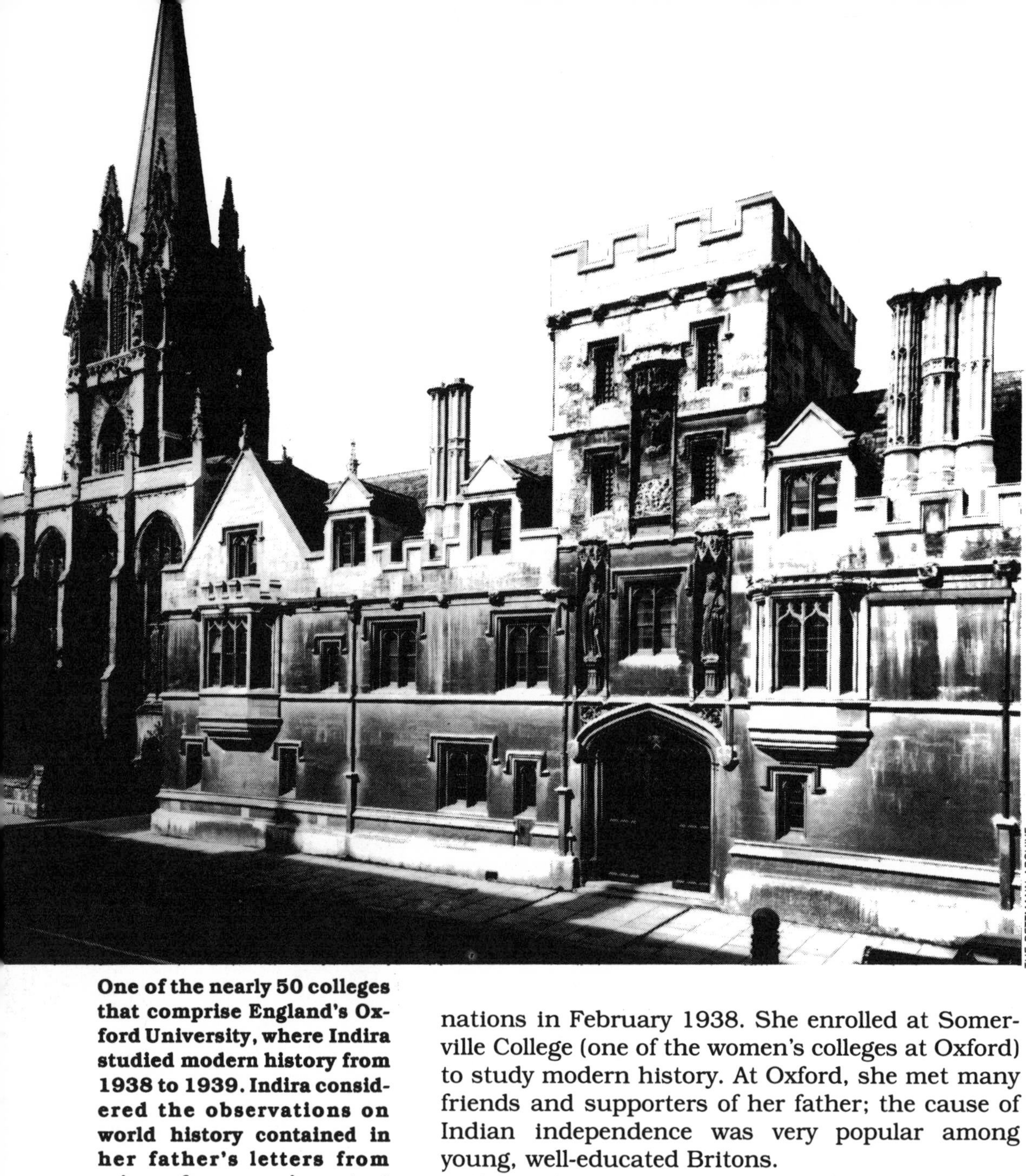

THE BETTMANN ARCHIVE

One of the nearly 50 colleges that comprise England's Oxford University, where Indira studied modern history from 1938 to 1939. Indira considered the observations on world history contained in her father's letters from prison far more important than anything she learned in school.

nations in February 1938. She enrolled at Somerville College (one of the women's colleges at Oxford) to study modern history. At Oxford, she met many friends and supporters of her father; the cause of Indian independence was very popular among young, well-educated Britons.

Although Indira was lonely at Oxford, she had one friend living nearby, Feroze Gandhi, a young Indian man, who was studying at the London School of Economics. Feroze Gandhi (no relation to Mohandas Gandhi) had known the Nehrus for some time, and had visited them often at Anand Bhavan and in Switzerland. He had even proposed marriage to Indira while she was at school in Poona, and one of the reasons he had come to London was to be near her. Together in a foreign country, surrounded by strangers to whom India was a strange and distant land, their romance blossomed.

A month after Indira began her studies at Oxford, Adolf Hitler, the fascist dictator of Germany, invaded Austria. Tensions in Europe grew almost daily: in Spain, a bloody civil war was raging between fascist rebels and the supporters of the elected government. In September 1938 Britain and France signed a pact with Germany whereby they abandoned Czechoslovakia — one of their allies — to the Germans without a fight. "Peace at any price" had become the philosophy of the British government. Nehru, who was on a five-month tour of Europe at the time, reacted angrily to the pact: "Peace at any price — at the price of the blood and suffering of others, the humiliation of democracy, and the dismemberment of friendly nations. Even so, it is not peace but continuous conflict, blackmail, the rule of violence, and ultimately war."

As it became increasingly apparent that a general European war was imminent, the movement for Indian independence seemed to lose steam. Although

German dictator Adolf Hitler (second from right; 1889–1945) and Italian dictator Benito Mussolini (right; 1883–1945) arrive in Munich, Germany, for a 1938 conference with British and French representatives. Britain and France's subsequent abandonment of Czechoslovakia to German domination convinced Nehru that peace had been bought "at the price of the humiliation of democracy."

UPI/BETTMANN NEWSPHOTOS

Nehru had said he was ready to fight the British if necessary, he realized that the fascist leaders — Hitler in Germany and Benito Mussolini in Italy — represented even more of a threat to the prospects for democracy in India. While in Europe, he flew to Spain and met with the leaders of the antifascist forces. Nehru refused invitations to meet with Hitler and Mussolini.

Meanwhile, Indira had gone to Switzerland to recover from a lung infection. When she returned to London in 1940, Britain was at war with Germany. Hitler's armies had already overrun much of Europe, and London was being attacked nightly by German bombers. Indira became a Red Cross volunteer, tending to air-raid casualties and driving an ambulance.

She is having training that is of far greater value than any she would have in a college. She is having training in the University of Nature.

—MOHANDAS GANDHI
discussing Indira's upbringing

Ironically, at the same time that Indira was helping the British during the bombing of London, her father was languishing in a British jail in India. Although Nehru's colleagues in the Congress shared his dislike of the fascists, they would not agree to let Indian soldiers fight alongside the British until Britain agreed to grant India its independence. More acts of civil disobedience followed the Congress's call for independence, to which the British responded by jailing Congress leaders.

In February 1941, after six years in Europe, Indira decided to return to India, even though she had not completed her degree at Oxford. Both Indira and Feroze Gandhi felt that they could be of more use back home. As their ship sailed down the coast of Africa, Indira and Feroze managed to smuggle all the profascist books out of the ship's library and throw them overboard.

When the ship docked at the South African port of Durban, Indira and Feroze toured the city. They were appalled by the poverty and miserable living conditions of Durban's black population. When the city's Indian community held a reception for Indira, she used the occasion to deliver a speech against the evils of segregation. She attacked not only the segregation practiced by the South African government, but the patronizing attitude of the prosperous Indian community toward the black majority.

AP/WIDE WORLD

A 1941 photograph of central London reveals the destruction caused by German air raids. Indira, who was in London at the height of the German bombing campaign against Britain, devoted much of her time to driving an ambulance and tending to the wounded.

7
Marriage and Prison

> *I don't think my being a woman makes any difference at all. It is a question again of putting people in compartments.*
> —INDIRA GANDHI

In December 1941, as the Japanese (who were now allied with Germany) marched toward India, the British government released the Congress leaders from jail. They hoped that Nehru and his colleagues could persuade the Indians to join them in the fight against the Japanese, but Nehru preferred the idea of free Indian units operating independently of the British army. Gandhi insisted that India should remain neutral. Some members of the Congress even encouraged Indians to join with the Japanese to throw out the British; British generals were shocked when some Indian soldiers captured by the Japanese did indeed change sides and take up arms against their former commanders.

In the midst of this national crisis, Indira surprised her father by telling him that she planned to marry Feroze Gandhi. Unlike Indira, who was born into a wealthy, well-educated family, Feroze came from a lower-middle-class background; furthermore, while Indira was a Hindu, Feroze belonged to a completely different religious group — the Parsis. By this time, Indira had become something of a celebrity in the nationalist movement, and many

AP/WIDE WORLD

Subhas Chandra Bose (1897–1945) declared himself head of an "Indian government in exile" during World War II. The Indian National Army (INA), which fought alongside the Japanese against the British, was largely composed of Indians recruited by Bose from Japanese prisoner-of-war camps.

Indira balances a basket presented by supporters during Republic Day (January 26) celebrations in 1968. India's constitution, adopted when the nation became a republic in 1950, guaranteed "*Justice*, social, economic and political; *liberty* of thought, expression, belief, faith and worship; *equality* of status and opportunity. . . ."

UPI/BETTMANN NEWSPHOTOS

Indians, particularly Hindus, reacted with anger to the news of her engagement. Nehru had always supported equal rights for Indians of all religions and ethnic groups, but the engagement strained even his capacity for tolerance. He found it difficult to overcome his instinctive prejudice, particularly where the future happiness of his only daughter was concerned.

Finally, Nehru asked Indira to consult Mohandas Gandhi. Gandhi questioned the young couple, and then gave his blessing to the marriage. According to Gandhi, mixed marriages between members of different races and religions were "bound to multiply with benefit to the society. At present we have not even reached the stage of mutual toleration." Although many in India still disapproved, Nehru finally agreed to the match, saying, "It is no business of parents or others to come in the way." Indira and Feroze Gandhi were married at Anand Bhavan on March 26, 1942. They spent their honeymoon in the beautiful valley of Kashmir in northern India.

In August 1942 the Congress issued a policy declaration known as the "Quit India" resolution,

Gandhi and Nehru confer in 1937, soon after Nehru had completed a 50,000-mile tour of India. Nehru said his homeland had reminded him of "some ancient [manuscript] on which layer upon layer of thought and reveries had been inscribed, and yet no succeeding layer had completely hidden or erased what had been written previously."

UPI/BETTMANN NEWSPHOTOS

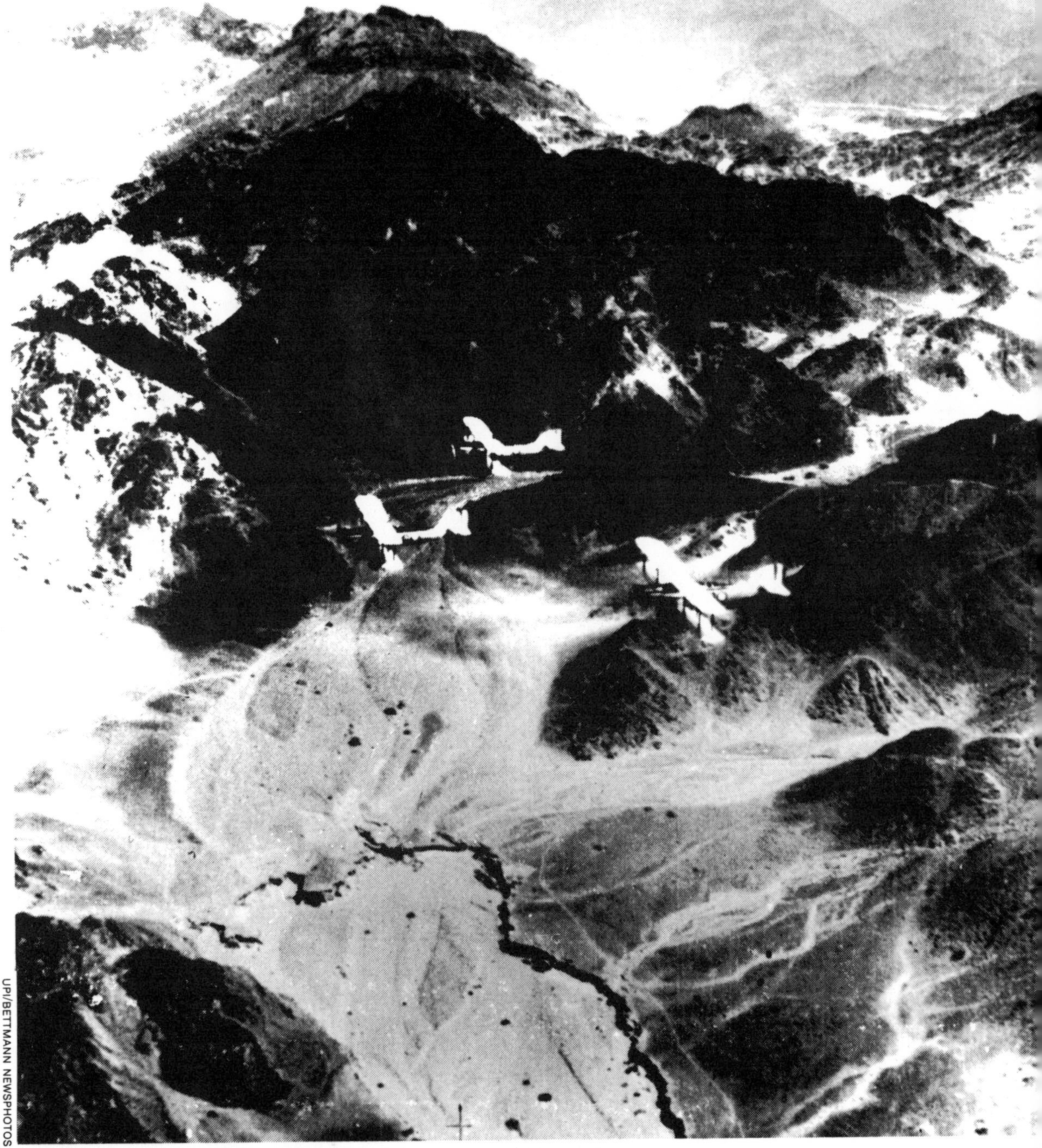

UPI/BETTMANN NEWSPHOTOS

British warplanes patrol the border between India and Afghanistan in 1939. Thousands of Indians were killed by machine guns carried by aircraft such as these in August 1942, when the Congress party's demand that the British withdraw from India provoked a violent response from the British military.

UPI/BETTMANN NEWSPHOTOS

Indira and Feroze are married in Allahabad on March 26, 1942. Despite the religious controversy stirred up by their decision to marry, the couple chose not to have a civil ceremony. Instead, they followed Vedic rites considered suitable for "mixed" marriages.

which called for the immediate withdrawal of the British from India. Congress then threatened a massive campaign of civil disobedience if the British refused to leave. Most of the Congress leaders, including Nehru and Gandhi, were promptly thrown in jail. Widespread strikes and protests quickly followed. The British, faced with the Japanese army on India's northeastern borders, were in no mood for civil disobedience; they responded to the revolt with armed force. As many as 10,000 Indians were killed by British troops, and at least 100,000 were arrested.

Back home in Allahabad, Indira and her new husband joined the protests. Indira was beaten by the police for carrying a Congress flag at a demonstration, and on September 10, while addressing a public meeting, she was arrested. Feroze, who tried to come to her aid, was arrested as well.

In the van on the way to jail, Indira continued her speech to the Indian policemen who had arrested her. They were so moved, she later wrote, that "they apologized, put their turbans at my feet and wept their sorrow because of what their job compelled them to do." She was put in the same cell as her aunt and her cousin, and the three women coped as best they could amid the mice, bats, and hordes of white ants that infested the prison.

The arrests resulted in a temporary halt to the demonstrations, and Indira was released in June 1943, after nine months in prison. (Her father, by this time, had spent almost nine *years* of his life in jail.) Feroze found a job selling insurance, and in August of the following year, Indira gave birth to her first child — a son, whom they named Rajiv. "To bring a new being into this world," Indira wrote, "to see its tiny perfection and to dream of its future greatness is the most moving of all experiences and fills me with wonder and exaltation."

Bombay demonstrators are engulfed by smoke from police bombs during the "Quit India" campaign of 1942. The British responded to the campaign, which called for their immediate withdrawal from India, with a brutal crackdown. More than 100,000 nationalists—including Nehru, Feroze, and Indira—had been imprisoned by November 1942.

AP/WIDE WORLD

8

A Bloody Independence

> ***Little did we guess that we would never see his wide toothless smile again, nor feel the glow of his protection.***
>
> —INDIRA GANDHI
> recalling her last visit to
> Mohandas Gandhi

World War II ended in victory for Britain and its allies, but political conditions in India had not improved, and many Congress leaders remained in prison. The British prime minister, Winston Churchill, was completely opposed to Indian independence. But in July 1945, to the surprise of many, Churchill and his Conservative party were defeated in the national elections by Clement Attlee and the Labour party. Attlee made Indian independence one of his government's top priorities. The Congress leaders were freed for the last time from British jails. After 30 long years of struggle, the day when India would be free of the British was finally in sight.

In September 1946 Nehru went to Delhi to take over as leader of the interim government. Meanwhile, Indira and Feroze moved to the northeastern city of Lucknow, where Feroze was to be managing editor of the *Herald*, a newspaper founded by Nehru in 1938. In December they had another son, Sanjay.

In Delhi, Nehru's negotiations with the British were complicated by a new and disturbing development: the leader of India's Muslim minority, a

AP/WIDE WORLD

As head of the Muslim League, Muhammad Ali Jinnah (1876–1948) was the political leader of India's 100 million Muslims. In 1946 Jinnah, who wanted India divided into separate Muslim and Hindu states upon independence, announced that he and his followers were "prepared to sacrifice anything and everything" to achieve their goal.

Indira jokes with her aunt, Vijayalakshmi Pandit (b. 1900), in New Delhi in 1966. The affectionate relationship between the two women was only marred once: in 1942 Vijayalakshmi, a well-to-do, high-caste Hindu, had expressed extreme disapproval of Indira's decision to marry Feroze, who was neither wealthy nor a Hindu.

AP/WIDE WORLD

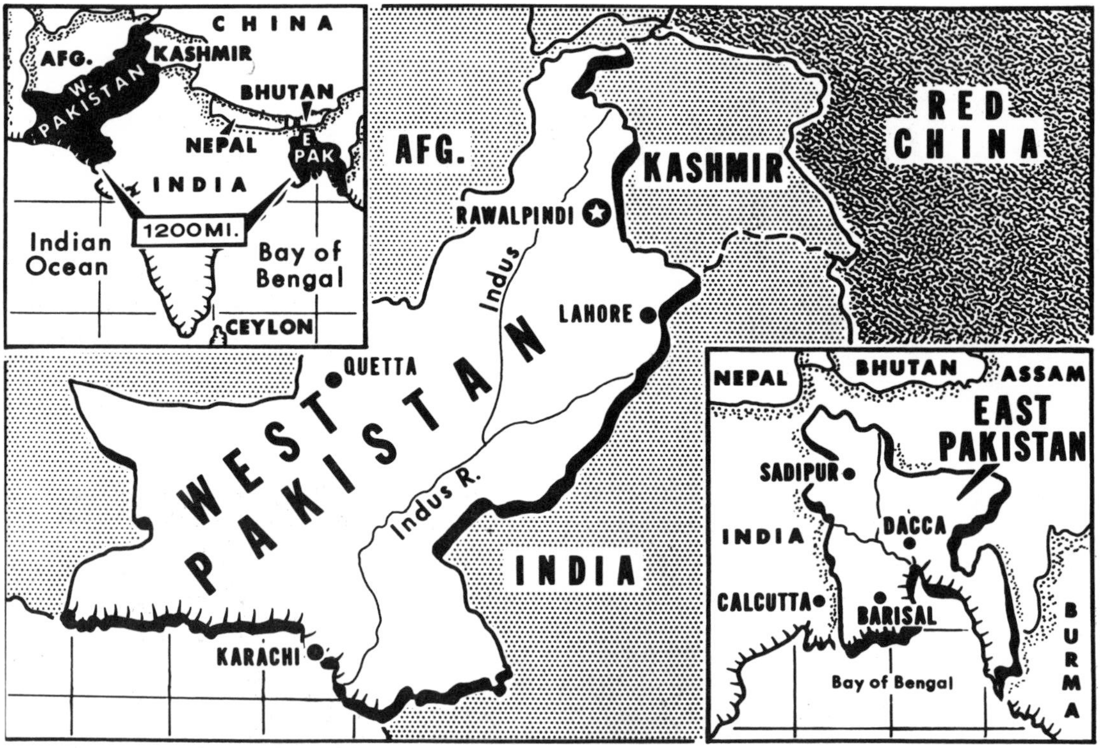

UPI/BETTMANN NEWSPHOTOS

A map shows the geographical disposition of India following independence. The new Muslim state of Pakistan consisted of two sections: West Pakistan, on India's northwestern border, and East Pakistan (now Bangladesh), on India's northeastern border.

lawyer named Muhammad Ali Jinnah, had been inciting his followers to riot and to commit acts of violence, particularly in those areas where Muslims were in the majority — the Punjab in the northwest and Bengal in the east. For centuries, India's two largest religious groups — the Hindus and the Muslims — had lived together as friends and neighbors, but, as independence approached, many Muslims feared that they would be discriminated against in an independent India. Toward the end of the 1930s, Jinnah had begun to use the Muslim League (which had been founded in 1906) as a platform for his attempt to create a mass movement among India's Muslims.

Gandhi, of course, was appalled by the widening rift between the Muslims and the Hindus; he had always imagined a united India, where Hindus, Muslims, and every other religious group would live together in harmony. Nehru, despite his qualms over his Parsi son-in-law, also supported freedom of religion and equal rights for all Indians. But many other Congress leaders felt that an independent India should be Hindu, since 83 percent of all Indians were Hindus. Jinnah's solution was to "partition" India, to divide it into two separate states: a Hindu nation called India, and a Muslim nation called Pakistan (which means "Land of the Pure"). Those areas in the Punjab and Bengal where Muslims were in the majority would become Pakistan, and the rest of India would remain under the control of the Hindus.

The new British viceroy — the World War II hero Lord Louis Mountbatten, who had been sent to India by King George VI to oversee the transition to independence — did not like the idea of a partitioned India, and neither did Gandhi or Nehru. But Jinnah's Muslim League continued to grow in strength, and in mid-1946, when elections were held for a constituent assembly, Nehru's hopes that Congress Muslims would defeat League Muslims in the contest for the seats reserved for Muslims were dashed. The 30 Muslim seats in the central assembly went to the League. Jinnah had thus demonstrated that Hindu-Muslim unity and Indian

Indians and sympathetic Britons celebrate India's independence on August 15, 1947. The farewell speech of the last viceroy, Lord Louis Mountbatten (1900–79), may have surprised some of his Indian listeners. Mountbatten called the historic day's events "a parting between friends, who have learned to honor and respect one another, even in disagreement."

UPI/BETTMANN NEWSPHOTOS

UPI/BETTMANN NEWSPHOTOS

Muslim refugees flee India for the new nation of Pakistan in September 1947. The partition of the subcontinent was followed by a massive bloodbath, which subsided only when Gandhi fasted in protest in January 1948.

independence were incompatible. To stress his point, he called for a Muslim League "Direct Action Day." On August 14, 1946, over 5,000 people died in Calcutta during a riot involving both Muslims and Hindus. Suddenly, villages where Hindus and Muslims had lived together for centuries erupted into violence, with gangs of Muslim fanatics slaughtering whole families of Hindus, and grief-stricken Hindus turning on innocent Muslim families in revenge.

By March 1947, Mountbatten and Nehru had reluctantly come to accept the idea of partition. Gandhi, however, refused to go along with the plan for a divided India. He traveled around the country, visiting villages where the bloodshed had been the worst and attempting to make peace between Hindus and Muslims. Despite Gandhi's efforts, however, tens of thousands of Indians continued to die, many at the hands of their neighbors.

Attlee and Mountbatten were determined to turn India over to the Indians by the fall of 1947, and British experts worked feverishly to draw up borders for Pakistan and to work out the details of the transfer of power from Britain to the Indian Constituent Assembly. Finally, at midnight on August 14, 1947, India became a free country, and Nehru became its first prime minister. The British flag that flew over the viceroy's palace was lowered, and the new Indian flag was raised. "Long ago we made a tryst with destiny," Nehru said in a speech to the cheering Constituent Assembly, "and now the time has come when we shall redeem our pledge. . . . It is fitting that at this solemn moment we take the pledge of dedication to the service of India and her people and to the still larger cause of humanity."

Even though it had now achieved independence, India still faced serious problems. There were millions of Hindus and Sikhs (a dominant religious group in parts of northwestern India) living within the borders of Pakistan, and hundreds of thousands of Muslims were living in India. During the next few months, one of the largest mass migrations in history took place: uprooted from their homes, over 12 million Indians made the long journey by foot — carrying all their belongings on their backs, or dragging them along in carts — to new and uncertain homes hundreds of miles away. Muslims from northern India fled to Pakistan, while Hindus and Sikhs from Pakistan fled to India. In the ensuing confrontations between Muslims and Hindus, more than 500,000 people were killed. The disturbances left 15 million homeless. Nehru, visiting the new border between India and Pakistan, said, "I have seen ghastly sights and I have heard of behavior by human beings which would disgrace brutes."

Indira did what she could to help the victims. She rescued one Muslim man who was about to be lynched, and protected another from an angry Hindu mob. At Gandhi's urging, she volunteered to work in Muslim neighborhoods, and encouraged

> ***I believe in the fundamental truth of all the religions of the world. I believe that they are all God-given.***
> —MOHANDAS GANDHI

UPI/BETTMANN NEWSPHOTOS

Gandhi embraces his granddaughters in September 1947. The religious violence produced by India's partition horrified Gandhi, who had always preached a message of tolerance. "Religions," he once wrote, "are different roads converging to the same point. What does it matter that we take different roads as long as we reach the same goal?"

Hindu and Muslim leaders to work out their differences peacefully. Sick at heart, Gandhi meanwhile worked tirelessly to end the violence. The city of Calcutta hovered on the edge of all-out war between the two groups; gangs of Hindus prowled the streets, killing any Muslims they saw.

Finally, in January 1948, the 78-year-old Gandhi announced that he would stage another fast: unless the Hindus and Muslims could learn to live together, he said, he would starve himself to death. After six days of fasting, Gandhi was so weak that he could barely speak; Nehru feared that he might die at any moment. At last, local Hindu and Muslim leaders came to his bedside and promised to stop the violence. Together, they begged him to eat. Once again, Gandhi's deep personal convictions had changed the lives of millions of Indians.

Only two days after he ended his fast, on January 30, 1948, Gandhi was shot and killed by a young Hindu fanatic. Indira had visited Gandhi the day before he was killed. Three-year-old Rajiv had placed a chain of flowers around the old man's big toe. "Little did we guess," she wrote, "that we would never see his wide toothless smile again, nor feel the glow of his protection."

The death of Gandhi was a particularly hard blow for Nehru, who had counted on having Gandhi's support and counsel in the struggle to create a new nation. In a radio broadcast, he told India that "the light that has illumined this country these many years will illumine it for many years to come, and a thousand years later that light will still be seen in this country and in the world." Only five months old, the new India had already been rocked by two great tragedies — the bloody violence between Hindus and Muslims, and the death of one of its greatest leaders.

United Nations delegates Sir Zafrullah Khan of Pakistan (left) and N. G. Ayyangar of India are stunned to read of Gandhi's assassination on January 30, 1948. Nehru, speaking in tribute to Gandhi, declared: "The light has gone out of our lives and darkness reigns everywhere. . . . Our beloved leader is no more."

UPI/BETTMANN NEWSPHOTOS

9

The First Prime Minister

Even the most Indian of our personalities were amalgams of East and West.
—INDIRA GANDHI

Indira found life in Lucknow, eight hours from Delhi by train, rather quiet after helping Gandhi during the riots and being at her father's side at the glorious moment when India won its independence. Toward the end of 1948, Indira decided that her father — and India — needed her more than her husband did, and she moved back to Delhi with her two young sons, leaving Feroze behind to manage the *Herald* by himself in Lucknow. The prime minister's mansion in Delhi was called *Teen Murti* House — "House of Three Statues." Indira made herself at home, quickly becoming her father's chief housekeeper, official hostess, secretary, and nurse.

Nehru turned 60 in 1949, and the burdens of his office weighed heavily upon him. He still felt keenly the loss of his father, his wife, and — most of all — Gandhi. Indira did what she could to make life easier for her father. Increasingly, she became his confidante and adviser, helping him deal with the enormous pressures and difficult decisions that a prime minister must face.

One of Nehru's biggest challenges was to develop

UPI/BETTMANN NEWSPHOTOS

Indira and Nehru meet with the president of Indonesia, Achmed Sukarno (1901–70) and Mrs. Sukarno in June 1950. Indira's sons, Rajiv (b. 1944) and Sanjay (1946–1980), are standing with the Sukarnos. Sukarno, like Nehru, had spent many years fighting colonial oppression: the Netherlands government recognized him as president of independent Indonesia in 1950.

U.S. President Dwight D. Eisenhower (1890–1969) greets Nehru and Indira in Washington, D.C., in 1956. Commenting on his relationship with leaders of the United States, Nehru said, "I want to be friendly with the Americans but always making it clear what we stand for. I want to make no commitments which come in the way of our basic policy."

UPI/BETTMANN NEWSPHOTOS

a foreign policy for India. As part of the British Empire, India had never needed a foreign policy — the British had represented India to the rest of the world. But a free India would become a major force in the new United Nations (this international organization had been formed in 1945) simply because of its enormous population: some 700 million, second only to China among the world's nations. Just like Gandhi, who had insisted during

Indira greets Zhou Enlai (1898–1976), prime minister of the People's Republic of China, at a reception in New Delhi in 1955. Zhou was to forfeit Nehru's trust and respect in 1962, when the Chinese army invaded India and annexed 16,000 square miles of its territory.

UPI/BETTMANN NEWSPHOTOS

World War II that India should remain neutral, Nehru favored a policy of "nonalignment." He hoped that India could become a mediator in international conflicts, and that it could speak for the other nations of the Third World (those nations, particularly former colonies in Africa, Asia, and South America, that were allied with neither the United States nor the Soviet Union). During his first years in office, Nehru traveled to the United States, Britain, Pakistan, China, and the Soviet Union, often with Indira at his side.

Because of the political struggle, my own childhood was an abnormal one, full of loneliness and insecurity.
—INDIRA GANDHI

In 1952 Feroze was elected as the Congress representative from Lucknow. He was now able to move to Delhi to be near his wife and children. Although he kept his own small apartment near the Parliament building, he spent most of his time at Teen Murti House with Indira and Nehru. Unfortunately, Feroze and Nehru differed on almost every subject, from matters of personal taste to the most important political issues of the day. Meals at the prime minister's mansion were often eaten in angry silence, or were interrupted by heated arguments between Feroze and Nehru.

In 1955 Indira — who by this time was widely known and respected by the Indian people — was nominated for membership on the Congress Working Committee, an important political post. She worked very hard on the committee, and in 1957 she received more votes than even Nehru himself for membership on the General Election Committee, which was responsible for selecting the candidates for the upcoming general election.

Indira had never run for the Congress, despite the urging of many of her friends and supporters. Her father had contributed to her political education and had helped her career as much as he could, but he knew that there would be grumblings from his political opponents if his daughter became a member of the Congress while he was still the prime minister. Nevertheless, Indira's political background could hardly have prepared her better for the job of a politician, and in 1959 she was elected president of the Congress — a post that her father and grandfather had held before her. Nehru accepted her election with good humor: "I am proud of her good nature, proud of her energy and work, and proud of her integrity and truthfulness. What she has inherited from me I do not know. Maybe she has inherited these qualities from her mother!"

Indira threw herself into the new job with her usual energy and enthusiasm. "The nation is in a hurry," she said at her first press conference, "and we can't afford to lose time. My complaint against the Congress is that it isn't going as fast as the people." But her first experiences with the actual workings of India's government were not very encouraging: India was still a nation of many different religious and ethnic groups, and the prevalence of factionalism made it difficult for the Congress to pass the sweeping social reforms that Indira favored. In addition, graft, bribery, and corruption were widespread among Indian politicians. Feroze had made his political reputation (and, in the process, embarrassed his father-in-law) by uncovering fraud in the Indian insurance industry, which had led to the resignation of Nehru's finance minister, T. T. Krishnamachari.

Once, [Indira] told me a sort of parable. Suppose your parents send you on a trip. They know there's a forest ahead and they teach you how to cross it. You come to the middle of the forest and there is a river across the way. Your parents foresaw the forest but they never foresaw the river. Unless, of your own accord, you learn how to swim there and then, you will have to turn back or die.

—NANDINI SATPATHI
chief minister of Orissa

In 1960 Feroze had a heart attack, and Indira, exhausted and dispirited by the petty squabbles of the Congress, resigned as president. She cared for Feroze during his illness, and when he was sufficiently recovered, he and Indira took a month-long second honeymoon in Kashmir in the far north. In September Feroze had a second, fatal heart attack; he was dead at the age of 48. The Gandhis' marriage had never been perfect, but Indira had loved her husband: "Conflict and unhappiness are not the worst things that can happen [in a marriage]," she said. "It is all the experiences one has that makes one what one is — the wider the experience, the stronger one's personality."

Because Nehru, now in his 70s, was suffering from kidney disease, Indira took over many of his duties, traveling all over India to campaign for the Congress party candidates who were running for Parliament. She also made many international trips on her father's behalf, to the United States, Europe, the Middle East, Africa, Japan and the Soviet Union.

On October 20, 1962, a major crisis erupted: the Chinese army invaded a barren stretch of uninhabited land on the border between India and China. Relations between India and the Chinese Communists had always been good, and when Chinese Prime Minister Zhou Enlai visited India in 1954, the two countries had pledged their mutual support. "The friendship of 960 million people," Zhou had said, "constitutes a mighty force for peace in Asia and the world." In 1959, however, the Chinese had invaded the mountainous country of Tibet on India's northeastern border. Much dismayed,

Students in New Delhi demonstrate against the 1962 Chinese invasion of India. During the conflict (in which India suffered a humiliating defeat), Indira made several visits to the battlefront to encourage the troops and comfort the civilian population.

UPI/BETTMANN NEWSPHOTOS

Nehru had nevertheless tried to remain on good terms with China.

When China demanded 16,000 square miles of Indian territory along the Chinese border, Nehru refused. The Chinese army invaded the territory in 1962, and the Indian army, which tried to defend the border, was badly beaten. If the Chinese troops had continued to advance, the Indians would have been helpless to stop them, but the Chinese had made their point, and stayed put. The war had lasted only a month; the land acquired by the Chinese was worthless, but they had demonstrated their military might to the world.

During the war, Indira made several trips to the front to encourage the Indian troops and to comfort the people who lived in the cities that lay in the path of the Chinese. Nehru, however, was badly humiliated by the Indian defeat. "I think he collapsed," said his defense minister, Krishna Menon. "It demoralized him completely."

Two years later, Nehru suffered a stroke. At the age of 74, he died on May 26, 1964.

A Chinese soldier faces his Indian counterpart across the border between their countries in 1967. Although the Sino-Indian War had been over for five years, relations between the two huge nations had remained tense.

UPI/BETTMANN NEWSPHOTOS

UPI/BETTMANN NEWSPHOTOS

Indira, newly elected president of the Congress party, faces the press on February 11, 1959. She had amused her colleagues by closing her first presidential address with lines from a popular Indian song: "We are the women of India / Don't imagine us as flower-maidens / We are the sparks in the fire."

10

The New Prime Minister

Indira, like John Kennedy, could describe herself as an idealist without illusion.
—M. CHALAPATHI RAU
Indian historian

Who would succeed Nehru as prime minister? In all of India, there was no one equal to him in popularity or political experience. No other Indian politician was as widely known, either in India or abroad. Who, besides Nehru, could command the votes, wield the political power, and keep India's many conflicting factions united in one great democracy?

That had been the issue before the secret meeting of Congress party leaders that took place in October 1963. (This group, known as the "Syndicate," was a powerful force in Indian politics.) Nehru's health was failing, and if the Congress party was to retain power in the wake of a national crisis like the war with China, a successor to Nehru had to be chosen. One possibility might have been Feroze Gandhi, had he lived. Indira herself was considered, but she was still young, and relatively inexperienced, and — perhaps more to the point — a woman. A third possibility was Morarji Desai, an ambitious and outspoken finance minister in Nehru's cabinet, who had openly disagreed with Nehru on the issue of

AP/WIDE WORLD

Lal Bahadur Shastri (1904–66), whom Indira succeeded as prime minister on January 19, 1966. Shastri, who had become extremely popular after his brilliant management of India's response to the 1965 Pakistani invasion, died while negotiating a peace treaty with Pakistan.

Prime Minister Indira Gandhi greets Indian President Sarvapelli Radhakrishnan (1888–1975) on February 13, 1967, just days after a political opponent's stone had broken her nose at a rally. She had deeply impressed her audience by continuing with her speech despite the pain she was suffering from the blow.

UPI/BETTMANN NEWSPHOTOS

nonalignment; but many of the party leaders distrusted Desai, and suspected him of being an agent of the U.S. Central Intelligence Agency. After much debate, the party leaders finally decided on Lal Bahadur Shastri. Shastri was likable and easygoing, and he was much more popular with the Indian public than the proud and uncompromising Desai. In the political maneuvering that followed Nehru's death, Desai — although he felt much better qualified for the job himself — reluctantly accepted the decision of the Syndicate, and agreed to support Shastri for prime minister.

Once in office, Shastri immediately offered Indira her choice of positions in his cabinet. He knew she was very popular in India, and he hoped that by giving her a cabinet post, he would increase public support for his administration. Many thought that Indira, with all her experience of representing her father abroad, would choose to be foreign minister, but instead she asked to be minister of information and broadcasting.

Indira moved from the prime minister's mansion into a smaller house. Her sons were both away at school, Sanjay in India and Rajiv in England. (When told she was being criticized for sending her son to school in England, Indira replied with typical independence, "I couldn't care less what people say.") Indira continued her father's practice of holding a *durbar*, or reception, early every morning; anyone, from the lowliest worker to the highest public official, could visit the house and ask for her help, her opinion, or her blessing.

Indira's previous experience in government had not been a pleasant one: she had been repelled by the corruption and the wheeling and dealing that were so much a part of Indian politics. She kept a low profile in Shastri's cabinet and in Parliament, but when she did speak out, she often enraged members of her own party. Indira complained bitterly that although the party leaders were willing to vote in favor of progressive resolutions supported by the majority, "in practice they see to it that decisions not to their liking are not implemented."

Indira continued to travel widely in India and

abroad. In 1964 she was the first important foreign visitor to the Soviet Union after Nikita Khrushchev, one of Russia's most flamboyant leaders, had been ousted by his more conservative colleagues. Before she left, she obtained reassurance from the new Soviet leaders of their country's continued goodwill toward India. Early in 1965, she flew to the southern state of Madras, whose mainly Tamil-speaking residents were violently protesting the adoption of Hindi as one of India's official languages. (The other official language was English.)

A few months later, in August 1965, Indira was visiting Kashmir when Pakistan launched a surprise attack on Srinagar, the capital of the region. Relations between India and the new nation of Pakistan had been strained ever since the violent days of the late 1940s. The Muslim leaders of Pakistan had never been satisfied with the division of territory, particularly when Kashmir became part of India. Pakistan hoped that a surprise attack, aided by Muslim sympathizers in Kashmir, would overwhelm the Indian defenses, but they had not counted on the speed and efficiency of the Indian government's response to the situation once it had recovered from its initial surprise.

Well, look, the big powers are all out for their own interests. We are not under an illusion that anybody is going out of his way to help us. Let's look at the war in Vietnam, for instance. Now that was not a stabilizing thing, was it?
—INDIRA GANDHI

Indira helped Kashmir's government to rally the Indian forces, keeping Shastri and his cabinet informed of every development. The invaders were soon pushed back over the border, and the embarrassed Pakistani leaders quickly agreed to a peace treaty with India.

Shastri, suddenly a national hero, made plans to reshuffle his cabinet and to choose his own ministers, much to the dismay of the party leaders. The good-natured Shastri had turned out to be more ambitious than they had expected. On December 31, 1965, Shastri left for the Soviet city of Tashkent, where he was to sign the peace treaty with Pakistan. But while still in Tashkent, Shastri suffered a heart attack and died. India once again plunged into grief and political confusion.

Desai quickly announced his intention to run for prime minister. The Syndicate however, still distrustful of Desai, picked a candidate whom they believed they would be able to control easily — Indira Gandhi. Events would later prove that the members of the Syndicate had badly underestimated Indira. Historian Tariq Ali has written that "[the Syndicate] had, without being aware of it, signed their own death warrants as politicians."

Desai campaigned vigorously against Indira, but the Syndicate's political connections and Indira's personal popularity prevailed. On January 19, 1966, Indira became India's third prime minister, the first woman to hold the post. Desai won enough votes to become Indira's foreign minister and deputy prime minister.

We want peace because there is another war to fight—the war against poverty and ignorance. We have promises to keep with our people—of work, food, clothing, and shelter, health and education.
—INDIRA GANDHI

Moving once again into Teen Murti House, Indira soon discovered that being a prime minister was quite unlike being president of the Congress or a member of the cabinet. For one thing, the Syndicate was now firmly in control of the Indian government. It had already made a number of political deals in Indira's name, deals that she was forced to honor. On the other hand, Indira had a fiercely independent nature, and was always ready to take her side of an issue to the people if she had to. As she told a journalist, "There is a question of whom the party wants and whom the people want. My position among the people is uncontested."

One of Indira's first acts as prime minister was to visit the United States. She hoped to persuade the Americans to provide much-needed foreign aid and investment. During her trip to Washington, President Lyndon B. Johnson agreed to an aid package that included 3.5 million tons of American wheat. Later, however, when Indira assured the Soviets that nonalignment was still India's policy and then made a statement condemning the American military presence in Vietnam, Johnson canceled the aid package. Suddenly, Indira was being attacked by both wings of her own party: the left, which favored stronger ties with the Soviet Union, and the right, (led by Desai), which wanted to improve relations with the United States. Once again, Indira turned to the people of India, addressing 160 public meetings and traveling some 15,000 miles during the first two months of 1967.

UPI/BETTMANN NEWSPHOTOS

Indira meets with U.S. President John F. Kennedy (1917–63) at the White House in 1962. Perhaps hoping to improve her chances of securing American aid for India, Indira once called Kennedy one of the three non-Indians she admired most.

Sometimes the crowds were hostile to Indira. At one stop, she was hit by a stone that fractured her nose. Holding a handkerchief against her face to stanch the bleeding, she spoke of India as a great family, portraying herself as its mother, and scolded her assailant for his action, which she considered an insult to India. Like Gandhi and her father, she was able to change the mood of the crowd simply through the force of her personality.

When several key party leaders failed to be reelected, the Syndicate began to realize that they had underestimated both Indira's popularity and her political skill. Desai continued to criticize her leadership in his usual abrasive way, but during the next five years Indira's popularity grew, and in 1969 she demonstrated her formidable mastery of politics by wresting control of the Congress party from the Syndicate.

Indira confers with her deputy prime minister, Morarji Desai (b. 1896), in early 1967. Desai, who had been Indira's main rival for the positions of Congress party leader and prime minister in 1966, led an unsuccessful intraparty revolt against her in 1969.

UPI/BETTMANN NEWSPHOTOS

UPI/BETTMANN NEWSPHOTOS

Indira speaks at a Congress party rally in 1972, a year in which appalling droughts brought increased hardship to more than 80 million Indians. The prime minister greatly resented her critics' charges that she paid too little attention to the problem of poverty.

Late in 1970, at the height of her popularity, Indira called for elections to be held in 1971, a year before they were scheduled to take place under the terms of the Indian constitution. She campaigned under the slogan "Remove Poverty!" (her opponents' rallying cry was "Remove Indira!"). She spoke to some 20 million voters at 410 public meetings in the first three months of 1971, and when the elections were held, Indira's Congress party won 352 of the 518 contested seats. The rival faction of the Congress party, headed by the Syndicate, won only 16 seats.

It was an immense personal victory for Indira. "The elections became a sort of movement," she wrote, "a people's movement . . . the peasant, the worker, and, above all, the youth, cut across all caste, religious and other barriers." At the same time, she realized how enormous the task ahead would be. Although she knew her substantial majority in the Congress would make some things easier, she also realized that some things would be more difficult.

11
The Second Term

> ***A 20th-century Mona Lisa, whose smile meant all things to all men.***
> —the *Chicago Times* describing Indira Gandhi

Indira had only 15 days in which to savor her reelection. On March 25, 1971, India was drawn into yet another international crisis — civil war in Pakistan. When the British mapmakers had drawn up the borders of Pakistan in 1947, they had divided it into two separate regions: West Pakistan, an area to the northwest of India that had been part of the Punjab; and East Pakistan, which had been the Muslim area of Bengal. The two regions were on opposite sides of India, almost 1,000 miles apart, which made it particularly difficult for the Muslim leaders to govern the new nation. West Pakistan was by far the wealthier of the two regions, and contained the seat of government, the bulk of the ruling class, and the army. Although 60 percent of Pakistan's population lived in the East, the residents of East Pakistan were crowded into a much smaller geographical area.

President Ayub Khan of Pakistan had resigned in the aftermath of the ill-fated 1965 invasion of Kashmir. In 1969, the government was taken over by General Yahya Khan, who declared martial law but promised free elections in 1970. In the December

UPI/BETTMANN NEWSPHOTOS

An East Pakistani policeman is held at gunpoint by a Bengali militiaman on December 20, 1972, four days after Pakistani forces in East Pakistan surrendered to the Indian army. After the Indian victory, East Pakistan's Bengali secessionists proclaimed their country the independent nation of Bangladesh.

Indira meets with U.S. President Richard M. Nixon (b. 1913) in Washington, D.C., in November 1971. Because the Indian government had criticized America's involvement in Vietnam and had also signed a friendship treaty with the Soviet Union, relations between the United States and India were deteriorating rapidly at this point.

UPI/BETTMANN NEWSPHOTOS

1970 voting, the East Pakistan presidential candidate Sheikh Mujibur Rahman, defeated the West Pakistan candidate, Zulfikar Ali Bhutto. Candidates from East Pakistan also won a majority in the National Assembly, which was to write a new constitution for Pakistan. Although this should have made Rahman the new president, the wealthy residents of West Pakistan had no wish to be governed by a prime minister from East Pakistan, especially one who had demanded a greater degree of self-government for the residents of his own region. Khan postponed the meeting of the National Assembly, and the residents of East Pakistan, feeling that they had been betrayed by West Pakistan, began a massive campaign of civil disobedience. On March 25, 1971, Khan sent the Pakistani army — which was made up almost entirely of West Pakistanis — to quell the riots and demonstrations in the East. Rahman was arrested and taken to West Pakistan. Thousands were killed in East Pakistan (which had declared itself the independent nation of Bangladesh) and some 10 million refugees fled over the border into India.

We are friends with the Soviet Union, although people [in America] have tended to read much more into our treaty of friendship and cooperation than is in it.

—INDIRA GANDHI

The situation placed India in a very difficult position. Although sympathetic to the plight of the East Pakistanis, it was reluctant to become involved in the civil war, since one of Pakistan's allies was China, and India did not want to risk another war with the Chinese. In addition, the United States was supporting West Pakistan, partly because of Indira's attack on the American involvement in Vietnam. Hoping to persuade China and the United States to stay out of the conflict, Indira visited Moscow and signed a treaty of peace and friendship with the Soviet Union — a major departure from her father's policy of nonalignment. She also visited Britain, Belgium, France, West Germany, Austria, and the United States to argue the case of East Pakistan and to plead for assistance for the millions of refugees.

India finally became involved in the conflict on December 3, 1971, when the Pakistani air force bombed eight Indian airfields. Pakistan had hoped the attack would discourage the Indian military from continuing its preparations for armed intervention in East Pakistan. Before long, Pakistani troops were once again crossing into Kashmir. The Indian government immediately declared war on Pakistan, and sent Indian troops into East Pakistan to fight the Pakistani army units there. The United States, to Indira's dismay, called India the aggressor, and ordered the Seventh Fleet into the Bay of Bengal as a warning to India to withdraw its troops. Meanwhile, the Soviet Union moved its own ships into the Bay of Bengal and declared that if China or the United States intervened, Soviet forces would come to India's defense.

The Indian army quickly surrounded the Pakistani troops in East Pakistan, and they surrendered on December 16. India recognized East Pakistan as the independent nation of Bangladesh, and Bangladesh severed all ties with West Pakistan. Rah-

Soviet leader Leonid I. Brezhnev (1906–82) welcomes Indira to Moscow in September 1971. When the Indo-Pakistan War broke out three months later, the U.S. government (which backed Pakistan) attempted to intimidate India by sending the U.S. Seventh Fleet into the Bay of Bengal. Brezhnev supported India by ordering Soviet vessels into the area.

UPI/BETTMANN NEWSPHOTOS

A dead Pakistani soldier lies sprawled in an East Pakistan trench in late 1971. The Indo-Pakistan War began on December 3, 1971, when Pakistan, fearing that India planned to intervene in the conflict between the Pakistani army and Bengali secessionists, ordered its air force to bomb eight Indian airfields.

UPI/BETTMANN NEWSPHOTOS

> ***A few years ago, people spoke of Mrs. Gandhi admiringly as "a modern mind," but now they speak of her disparagingly as "the Empress," "the Lady," "Madame," or simply "she."***
>
> —VED MEHTA
> Indian historian

man, released from prison, became the leader of the new nation. Meanwhile, Bhutto, who had lost the election to Rahman, was elected president of Pakistan.

Much of the credit for winning the war with Pakistan — and for avoiding superpower involvement in the conflict — belonged to Indira. Although Indira's popularity was soaring, her campaign to "Remove Poverty" had done very little to improve conditions in India. A severe drought in 1972, followed by floods, had caused widespread food shortages. The war itself had been very costly, and it was just as expensive to feed and house the 10 million refugees from Bangladesh. Inflation seemed to be out of control: prices rose by 22 percent in 1973, and by 30 percent in 1974. Like many Third World countries, India was faced with a huge deficit and foreign debt, and when Indira tried to ease the problem by restricting imports, the hardships and shortages increased.

Workers all over India protested the worsening conditions. In Bombay, there were over 12,000 strikes in just 18 months. The worst strike occurred in April 1974, when the railway unions voted to bring all of India's trains to a halt. Declaring the strike illegal, the government arrested thousands of strikers, dismissed the union leaders, and even burned the homes of strikers and terrorized their families. Indira succeeded in breaking the strike, but her popularity suffered.

Indira's political opponents were faced with a problem similar to the one that had confronted the Syndicate after the death of Nehru. Who had the

A view of a New Delhi slum attests to the appalling conditions in which most Indians live. Indira's "Remove Poverty" campaign (which she initiated in 1971, when 40 percent of all Indians were living on less than 12 cents a day), failed because of middle-class resistance to increased taxation.

UPI/BETTMANN NEWSPHOTOS

charisma, the visibility, and the political experience to challenge Indira in the national elections? This problem was solved in 1974, when 71-year-old Jaya Prakash Narayan spoke out against Indira's government. A friend and colleague of Nehru, Narayan had disagreed with some of Nehru's policies back in 1936, and had resigned from the Congress. Now, almost 40 years later, Narayan was urging Indians to begin a new campaign of civil disobedience against the government; he urged a return to the India of a century ago, when Indian life was centered around small, rural villages instead of around a huge government bureaucracy in Delhi. To many Indians, this seemed like a good idea — the corruption in Indira's government was well known, and Indira herself had been criticized for setting up her son Sanjay as head of an automobile factory at public expense.

Mrs. Gandhi is worse than Hitler or Stalin.

—MORARJI DESAI
opposition leader and
Indian prime minister, 1977–79

As Narayan's "Total Revolution" campaign grew in popularity, Indira received another political blow: the High Court in Allahabad found her guilty of election fraud. The fraud was minor — Indira had used government vehicles and employees during her 1971 reelection campaign — but the opposition leaders called for her resignation, and so did the Indian press. Even some members of her own party felt she should step down; they began a quiet search for a successor.

Narayan attacked the corruption and inefficiency of Indira's government, and called for a week of demonstrations outside her home, beginning on June 29, 1975. Hundreds of thousands of people were expected to participate, but the demonstrations never took place. Meeting privately with her closest political allies, Indira decided that the only way to retain control of the government was to suspend key provisions of the constitution, including freedom of speech, freedom of the press, and the right to strike. Narayan was arrested, and his demonstrations were canceled. On June 26, 1975, Indira Gandhi — the democratically elected prime minister of a free nation — became a virtual dictator, with powers far beyond even those once held by the British viceroy.

UPI/BETTMANN NEWSPHOTOS

Jaya Prakash Narayan (1902–79) waves to cheering supporters at a March 1975 demonstration protesting Indira's policies. Narayan, a disciple of Gandhi and an opponent of industrialization, was an outspoken critic of the corruption that had become rampant among government officials during Indira's premiership.

कांग्रेस अध्यक्ष

12

The State of Emergency

> ***India, the land of every seventh person in the world, became virtually a continent of silence on June 26, 1975, when Indira Gandhi's government proclaimed a state of emergency.***
> —VED MEHTA
> Indian historian

Indira's proclamation of emergency declared: "The security of India is threatened by internal disturbances." India had proclaimed a state of emergency before, during wars and when the nation itself was in danger, but the only real danger in 1975 was that Indira Gandhi and her Congress party might be unseated.

All Indira's opponents, including Narayan and Desai, were jailed, along with many of their followers. Wages were frozen, and all strikes and protests were banned. The Indian press was censored, and foreign journalists who wrote articles critical of Indira's government were ordered to leave the country at once.

It was a dark time for India. The state of emergency was widely condemned; one of India's allies, the Soviet Union, however, was pleased that Indira had taken action to stabilize her country. There was some support for the state of emergency in India, particularly from wealthy businessmen who had been concerned about the recent strikes and demonstrations, and from corrupt politicians, who were delighted by the idea of staying in power without

UPI/BETTMANN NEWSPHOTOS

An untouchable child gazes at a statue of Gandhi in December 1976, when Indian democracy—for which Gandhi had lived and died—was still in suspension due to the state of emergency.

Convinced that her government was about to be unseated by a coalition of her opponents, Indira announced on June 26, 1975, that the "security of India [was] threatened by internal disturbances." She then proclaimed a state of emergency, initiated press censorship, banned all strikes, and had 100,000 of her opponents arrested.

UPI/BETTMANN NEWSPHOTOS

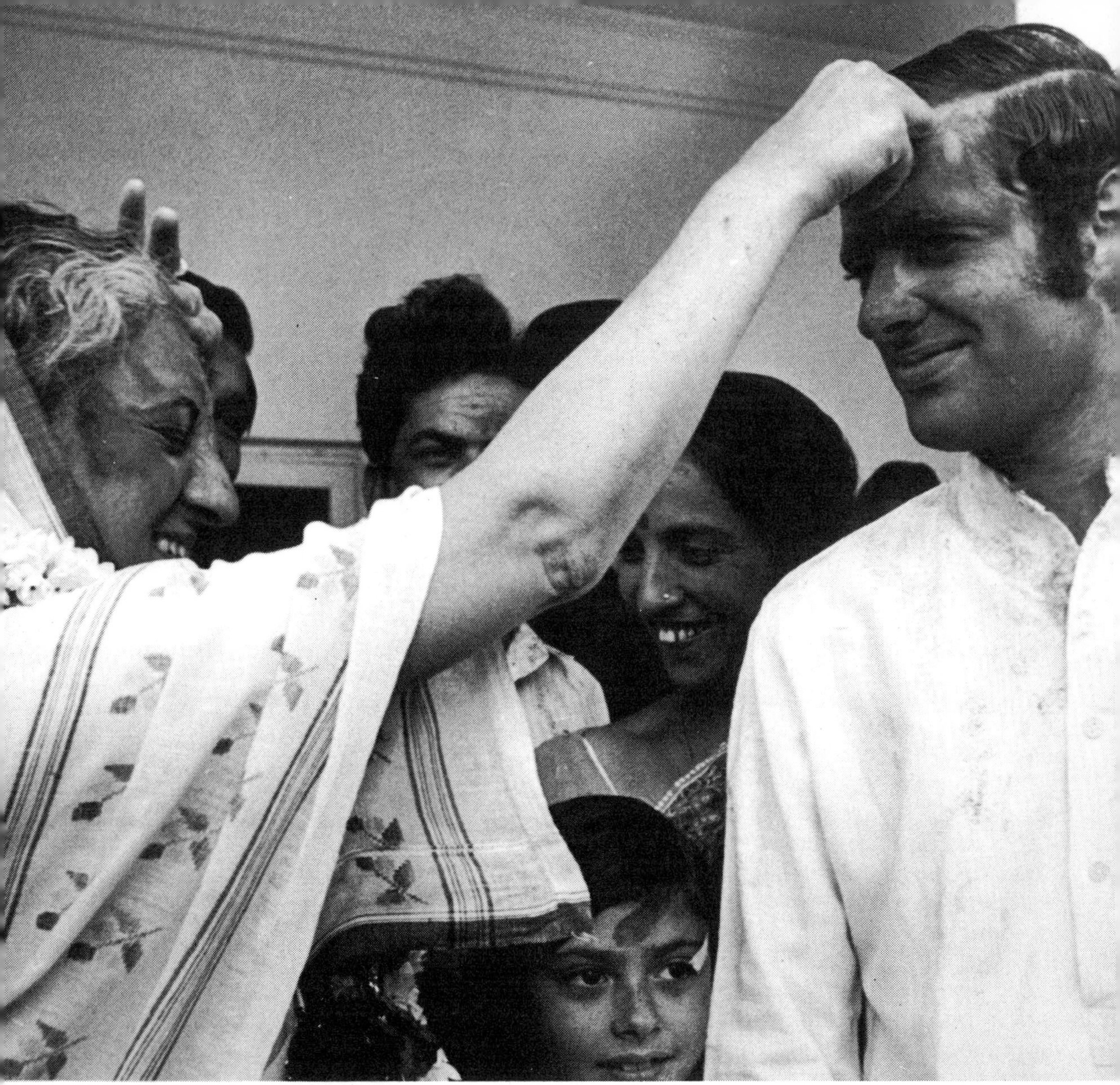

UPI/BETTMANN NEWSPHOTOS

Indira ritually anoints her son Sanjay during a Hindu festival. Although Sanjay had no official position in the government, he became his mother's most influential adviser during the state of emergency. His hasty and often brutal methods of effecting social change alienated many of Indira's previously loyal supporters.

having to run for reelection. "Things had gone too far," said one powerful industrialist. "You can't imagine what we've been through here — strikes, boycotts, demonstrations . . . the parliamentary system is not suited to our needs." Most of Indira's Congress party supported the state of emergency; those who did not were quickly jailed.

The state of emergency failed to solve any of the problems that Indira claimed to be worried about:

poverty, inflation, and the enormous foreign debt. Although the state-controlled media had a lot to say about the prime minister's "20-point program" of domestic economic reforms, the source of India's problems lay much deeper than Indira was willing to dig. As one Indian economist said, "The root cause of the present inflation is the attempt to eliminate poverty without touching the rich, without even calling a temporary halt to the extravagance of the government and the affluence of the few."

During the state of emergency, Indira's younger son, Sanjay, became not only one of her strongest supporters and most trusted advisers, but, in the eyes of many, her obvious successor. Sanjay, however, rarely managed to finish what he started, despite the fact that he was by nature both energetic and ambitious. He had failed to graduate from the Doon School, the prestigious Indian prep school that his older brother, Rajiv, had attended before going on to Cambridge. Although he was passionately interested in automobiles, he had dropped out of a three-year management training program at the Rolls-Royce auto factory in England. His scheme to manufacture a low-priced Indian automobile called the Maruti, bankrolled by the government, had been another expensive failure. While Rajiv — who was a pilot for Air India — did all he could to distance himself from his mother's politics, Sanjay became Indira's most outspoken — and controversial — supporter. He had his own program for social reform, among whose priorities were the clearance of city slums, reforestation, the elimination of the dowry system, and — perhaps the most critical and controversial element of his program — the forceful imposition of birth control through a campaign of mass sterilization.

Democracy meant responsibility, not license for everyone. The government's responsibility was to allow freedom of speech and association, but the opposition and citizens had also the responsibility of not paralyzing government functioning.
—INDIRA GANDHI
on the state of emergency

Birth control was a serious problem in a nation of 700 million, but because sons were so highly valued in Indian society, previous attempts to introduce birth control to the Indian public had met with strong resistance. Sanjay's solution to the problem of popular resistance to birth control was direct: medical teams, accompanied by police escorts, traveled around the countryside in vans, kidnapping

New Delhi businessmen campaign against India's ancient dowry system. The protest followed increased reports of brides being burned to death by the families of bridegrooms who were not satisfied with the dowries (payments) brought by their new wives. Indira's son Sanjay was a leader of the movement to abolish the dowry system.

UPI/BETTMANN NEWSPHOTOS

BURN
DOWREY
NOT
BRIDE
LIONS CLUB OF
GREATER DELHI

[Sanjay Gandhi] was quite ruthless. People who crossed his path were shown absolutely no mercy.

—KHUSHWANT SINGH
Indian journalist

Indian men and performing vasectomies upon them whether they wanted the sterilization operation or not.

Sanjay's notion of slum clearance was as brutal as his birth-control campaign. Promising to construct new housing, he ordered the destruction of whole Muslim neighborhoods in Delhi. When one group of Muslims tried to stop the demolition crews from destroying their homes, the police fired into the crowd, killing 12 and injuring many more.

Sanjay's reform program enraged many Indians. They found it hard to believe that the grandson of Jawaharlal Nehru had so few qualms about alienating the entire population. Indira refused to hear any criticism of her son: "Those who attack Sanjay attack me," she insisted. At the same time, Indira realized that power was slipping away from her, and that the state of emergency could not be sustained forever. India's economic crisis remained desperate, and even with more than 100,000 of her critics and political rivals in jail, Indira continued to be attacked from all sides. Another cause for concern was the Indian army, which Indira had been using to suppress strikes and demonstrations. Indira real-

UPI/BETTMANN NEWSPHOTOS

Indira talks with Indian troops in the Punjab in 1971. Throughout the state of emergency, she used the Indian army (whose commanders fully supported her decision to suspend the democratic process) as a state police force, deploying it against strikers and demonstrators.

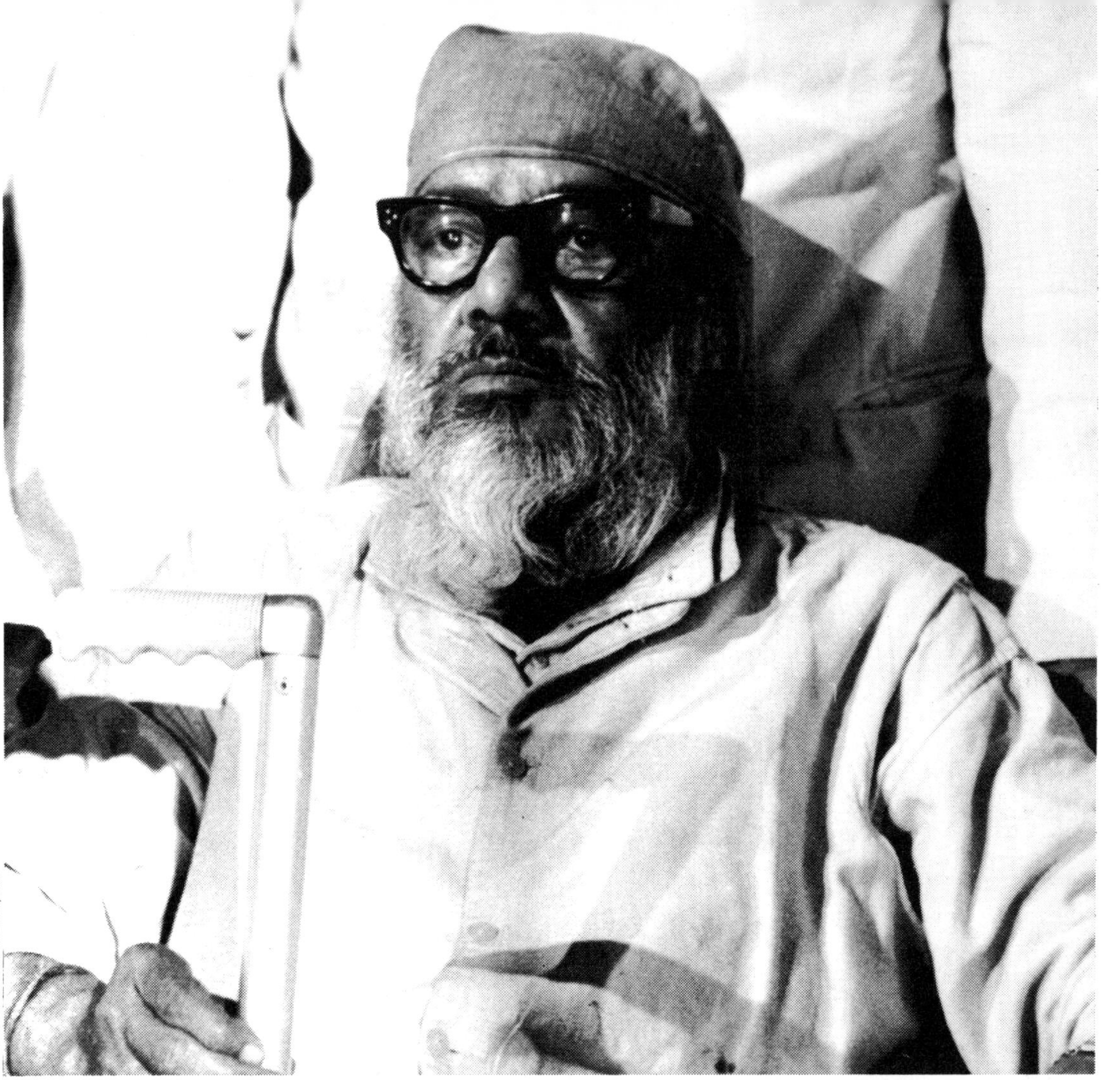

UPI/BETTMANN NEWSPHOTOS

Indian politician Raj Narain was defeated by 100,000 votes when he ran against Indira in her home constituency of Rae Bareilly in 1970. His resounding 1977 victory over Indira demonstrated the depth of the public's unhappiness with the state of emergency she had imposed.

ized that, even though her policies were popular with the military, worsening economic conditions could prompt the army leaders to seize control of the government in a military coup.

With no real hope of reelection, Indira, much to Sanjay's dismay, relaxed the state of emergency in 1977. She released her enemies from prison, and announced a new election for March 21. Over 200 million voters (60 percent of the electorate) turned out; Indira's Congress party was overwhelmingly defeated by a coalition party made up of her many rivals, and both she and Sanjay lost their seats in Parliament. Indira's 11-year reign as prime minister and then dictator had — at least for the moment — come to an end.

13

The Third Term

To many, Indira Gandhi remains a magnetic, enigmatic, and fascinating personality while to others, she is a sinister specter hovering in the political wings.
—MARY C. CARRAS
American historian

Indira was clearly out of power after the 1977 elections; unclear, however, was who was now *in* power. The public had gone to the polls not so much to vote for any particular candidate as to vote *against* Indira and Sanjay.

When Indira had announced the state of emergency, one of her chief worries was that a political alliance might be formed between Jaya Prakash Narayan, with his back-to-the-roots "Total Revolution" movement, and the fanatical, right-wing Hindu group known as *Jan Sangh* (Organization of the People). The Jan Sangh's program called for "one country, one nation, one culture, and the rule of the law" — in other words, anyone who was not a Hindu did not belong. The policies of the Jan Sangh, whose members considered even Nehru to have been a left-wing "Muslim appeaser," alarmed the millions of citizens in India's many minority groups.

Indira's worst fears had come to pass when she ended the state of emergency and let her opponents out of jail. Narayan and the Jan Sangh did form an alliance, and almost every other political faction in India joined the coalition against Indira: her old

UPI/BETTMANN NEWSPHOTOS

Jagjivan Ram (left), leader of India's untouchables, and Jaya Prakash Narayan, head of the *Janata* (People's) party, confer in New Delhi in February 1977. The Janata party, a coalition of leftist and rightist groups united only by their common hatred of Indira and the Congress party, triumphed at the polls on March 21, 1977.

Indira embraces her grandson, Rahul Gandhi (b. 1969), the first child of Rajiv Gandhi and Sonia Mainoo, whom Rajiv married in 1968. Too busy as prime minister to concentrate on her family or her hobbies, Indira was able to devote herself to such pursuits after her 1977 electoral defeat.

AP/WIDE WORLD

rival Desai, her enemies in the Congress party, a right-wing coalition called the *Bharatiya Lok Dal* (Indian People's Organization), the left-wing Socialist party (whose leader, George Fernandes, had been one of the jailed leaders of the railway strike), and last but not least, Jagjivan Ram, the powerful leader of India's untouchables. This rather unlikely coalition called itself the *Janata* party.

After soundly defeating Indira in the election, the Janata party's first order of business was the selection of a new prime minister. Narayan, as head of the party, was asked to choose from three candidates: Ram, leader of the untouchables; Charan Singh, leader of the Bharatiya Lok Dal; and Desai. Narayan picked the 81-year-old Desai. After being twice defeated for prime minister — first by Shastri in 1964, and then by Indira in 1966 — Desai had finally secured the office he had coveted since Nehru's death.

The various factions of the Janata party found it extremely difficult to achieve anything resembling consensus. Singh accused Desai's son of corruption, and Desai responded with personal attacks on Singh. (In fact, corruption was so widespread in Indian politics that the politicans hardly took the trouble to hide it.) Compromising photographs of Ram's son were published in a national magazine. The former opposition leaders were still behaving like the opposition, even though they were now the government; when they were not attacking each other, they were denouncing Indira's personality and policies as though she were still in office.

Please do not destroy the foundations that the fathers of the nation, including your noble father, have laid down. There is nothing but strife and suffering along the path you have taken.

—JAYA PRAKASH NARAYAN
long-time political
opponent of Indira Gandhi

Indira, who had meanwhile moved into a new house in Delhi, spent her days working in the garden and playing with her grandchildren. Before long, she revived the morning *durbar*, where she received a constant stream of Indians, most of whom had come to complain about the quarrelsome and ineffectual Janata government. She also did what she could to help her own wing of the Congress party — which was known as Congress (I) — get back on its feet.

In November 1978 Indira ran for a vacant Congress seat in the southern city of Karnataka. She

UPI/BETTMANN NEWSPHOTOS

Appointed prime minister of India after the Janata party's victory in the 1977 national elections, Morarji Desai would have little time to enjoy the position he had coveted since Nehru's death. Desai's enemies within the Janata party ousted him in 1979.

won by a landslide, throwing the Janata government into a panic. First, they had her arrested, and Indira and Sanjay spent a week in jail. Next, a parliamentary committee claimed to find some irregularities in the voting procedures, and rejected the results.

It was becoming increasingly apparent that keeping Indira out of office was the only policy upon

Sanjay Gandhi (foreground) and supporters of his Youth Congress movement are beaten to the ground by New Delhi policemen in May 1979. Sanjay and his followers were protesting the Janata government's plan to establish special courts to try people accused of committing "excesses" during the state of emergency.

which the government was united. On July 27, 1979, Desai was ousted from office by rivals in his own party, but even after much heated debate, the Janata leaders found that they could not agree on a replacement. Reluctantly, they announced new elections for January 3, 1980.

Now 62 years old, Indira used her proven strategy of round-the-clock campaigning, averaging 20 speeches a day and covering over 400,000 miles in her private helicopter. Sanjay and dozens of his po-

UPI/BETTMANN NEWSPHOTOS

UPI/BETTMANN NEWSPHOTOS

Sanjay and Indira in January 1980, six months before his death. His supporters' efforts to heroize their deceased leader were described by historian Tariq Ali as a "cynical attempt by the [members of Parliament] who were personally beholden to him to make doubly sure that their privileges would not come to an end."

litical cronies campaigned for contested parliamentary seats all over the country. Fewer than three years had passed since the end of the state of emergency, but Indian voters had already begun to think nostalgically of Indira's government, which at least had not been bogged down in petty quarrels.

To no one's surprise, Indira's party won the election; Congress (I) took 351 of the 542 seats in Parliament. Indira and Sanjay were back in business.

14

Indira's Successor

If I die today, every drop of my blood will invigorate the nation.
—INDIRA GANDHI
the night before her assassination

Indira and Sanjay moved quickly to consolidate their power in Congress (I), Parliament, and with the state governments throughout India. One of their chief priorities was to halt inflation, which Indira believed to be responsible for many of India's domestic problems. But on June 23, 1980 — only five months after Indira's return to power — Sanjay was killed while flying his small private plane. He had lost control of the aircraft while performing aerobatics, and had crashed into a field in Delhi. With Sanjay's death, Indira's hopes and plans for a political dynasty — a dynasty that had begun almost a century earlier with her grandfather Motilal — appeared to have been destroyed.

There was a great deal of genuine sympathy for Indira (and for Sanjay's widow and infant son), but many Indians — particularly the victims of Sanjay's mass sterilization and slum clearance programs — considered his death a blessing. Indira, although devastated by her loss, had little time to mourn. Sanjay had been not only her son, close friend, and adviser, he had been a crucial part of her government, and the leader of his own influential faction

UPI/BETTMANN NEWSPHOTOS

Two years after Sanjay's death, his widow, Maneka (b. 1956), announces the formation of the National Sanjay Organization. Maneka's last name—Gandhi—lent strength to her new political party, which was firmly opposed to Indira and the Congress party.

Indira and her son Rajiv confer in New Delhi in October 1984. After his 1983 election to Parliament, Rajiv, a former airline pilot, talked with a journalist about his new political career. "It will be satisfying to make progress," he said, "but I have no illusions about the difficulties."

UPI/BETTMANN NEWSPHOTOS

in Parliament. Who would fill the gap caused by Sanjay's untimely death? Even more importantly, who would now become Indira's successor to the prime ministership? By this time, the prospect of a prime minister who was neither a Nehru nor a Gandhi was almost inconceivable to many Indians.

Sanjay's widow, Maneka, announced that she was ready to take her husband's seat in Congress, but those (including Indira) who knew her best felt that Maneka was even more impractical and headstrong than Sanjay had been. Indira decided that only one person could possibly take Sanjay's place — his older brother, Rajiv.

Too much has been made, by some, of her childhood infatuation with Joan of Arc. She neither desired nor enjoyed martyrdom. Her primary interest lay in the exercise of political power.

—TARIQ ALI
Indian historian

Indira's eldest son, however, had no interest in politics. He enjoyed flying for Air India and did not relish the idea of forsaking his comfortable, suburban life with his Italian wife, Sonia, and their eight-year-old son, Rahul, for the uncertainties of a political career. Although Rajiv and Sonia got along well with Indira, they had both been disturbed by Sanjay's political escapades, and had never been fond of Sanjay's outspoken and assertive wife. Rajiv was by far the better educated of Indira's two sons, but his quiet and dignified temperament did not seem to suit him for the role of Indira's eventual successor.

After Sanjay's death, Indira pleaded with Rajiv to take a position in government. In Indira's opinion, the fate of India was closely tied to the fate of her own family — how could she govern India without an "heir apparent" at her side?

In August 1980 a group of 300 Congress (I) party leaders visited Rajiv and begged him to run for his dead brother's seat in Parliament. Rajiv and Sonia took several months to make up their minds. Finally, Rajiv agreed to campaign for Sanjay's old seat. He won by an overwhelming majority in June 1981.

Furious, Sanjay's widow announced that she would run against Rajiv herself; she was even angrier when she discovered that according to law, she was not old enough to run for office. Maneka quarreled publicly with Indira over Sanjay's estate, and in March 1982 she stormed out of the prime minister's mansion with her son, Feroze, whom she refused to let Indira see. Before long, she had formed her own political party — the National Sanjay Organization — and had joined forces with the opposition to Indira.

Rajiv turned out to be a surprisingly effective politician. Instead of blaming India's enormous social and economic problems on his political opponents, he tried (as he told a reporter) to "attract a new breed of person to politics — intelligent, Westernized young men with non-feudal, non-criminal ideas, who want to make India prosper rather than merely themselves." It was an uphill battle — young men who had won seats in Parliament by following his brother Sanjay seemed to have little interest in Rajiv's ideas, and were more concerned with their own status and well-being.

Indira faced her last and greatest crisis in the Punjab city of Amritsar, where the massacre in the Jallianwalla Bagh park had taken place in 1919. The Punjab was the home of India's fourth largest religious group, the Sikhs. A proud and warlike people,

The Indian army's elite Sikh Regiment parades in New Delhi in January 1984. The Sikhs, who constitute India's fourth largest religious group, are natives of the Punjab; celebrated for their military prowess, Sikh males are the backbone of the Indian army.

REUTERS/BETTMANN NEWSPHOTOS

the Sikhs had been valued as soldiers by the British army during the 19th century, and still dominated the Indian army a century later.

In 1947 the Sikhs had rejected Muslim rule for the Punjab. They had supported the partition of the subcontinent into the nations of Pakistan and India, even though the new borders would cut through some of their richest farmland and leave several of their holiest shrines in the hands of the Muslims. In 1966 Indira's government had agreed to the Sikhs' request that Punjabi — the language spoken by almost all Sikhs — be made the official language of the region. This had angered the Jan Sangh, which favored Hindi as the official language of all India; three of Indira's Congress (I) party members had been burned to death by Jan Sangh supporters in a town near Delhi. Finally, to appease the Jan Sangh, Indira had created a separate Hindu state in the Punjab called Haryana, but this in turn had infuriated the Sikhs. Many Sikhs who had supported the Congress (I) party now turned to the Sikhs' rights party, the *Akali Dal* (the Party of Immortals).

In the early 1980s, an even more militant Sikh organization emerged, a terrorist faction that demanded complete independence for the Punjab and the creation of a new Sikh state called Khalistan. The leader of this group, Jarnail Singh Bhindranwale, openly defied the government; his motorcycle gangs roamed the countryside, murdering anyone who opposed him.

Indira was reluctant to take any action against these terrorists for two reasons: first, Bhindranwale and his heavily armed followers had established a stronghold in Amritsar's Golden Temple, a Sikh shrine that was off-limits to the Indian police. Also, Indira hoped that the more moderate *Akali Dal* would expel the terrorists from the temple without assistance from the central government. Bhindranwale's brazen acts of terrorism, however, soon threatened to spark a civil war between the Sikhs and the Hindus in the Punjab.

Indira finally took action on the night of June 5, 1984. Indian army commandos stormed the Golden

REUTERS/BETTMANN NEWSPHOTOS

The Golden Temple, the Sikhs' most revered shrine, was used by a militant Sikh organization as a base for terrorist operations during the early 1980s. On June 5, 1984, Indian army commandos stormed the Amritsar temple on Indira's orders, killing the militants' leader and 1,000 of his followers.

Temple, and brought out the moderate Sikhs who lived and worked there. The next morning, the army attacked that part of the temple where Bhindranwale and his followers were hiding. By the end of the day, the army had lost several hundred men, but nearly 1,000 Sikh militants had been killed, including Bhindranwale, who was found with a machine gun cradled in his arms. Indira had made the mistake of turning Bhindranwale into a martyr: the Sikhs began to speak of him as a great hero, and the movement for a separate Sikh state grew in strength.

On the morning of October 31, 1984, four months after the battle at the Golden Temple, Indira was en route to her office with two of her bodyguards, both Sikhs. Uneasy about the presence of Sikhs in the prime minister's security force, Rajiv had suggested transferring the two men to other duties, but Indira

UPI/BETTMANN NEWSPHOTOS

Rajiv (second from left) and other members of the Gandhi family attend Indira's cremation on November 3, 1984. Indira, who had known that using force to dislodge Sikh terrorists from the Golden Temple might put her own life at risk, was assassinated by her Sikh bodyguards on October 31.

had laughed at his suspicions. She pointed out that they had guarded her for years. Furthermore, she asked, "How can we punish a whole community for what some minority has done?"

As Indira approached her office, the two guards swung their machine guns toward her and opened fire. Mortally wounded, she fell to the ground. The guns continued their deadly hail, and in a matter of seconds, Indira Gandhi was dead.

News of Indira's assassination struck the nation

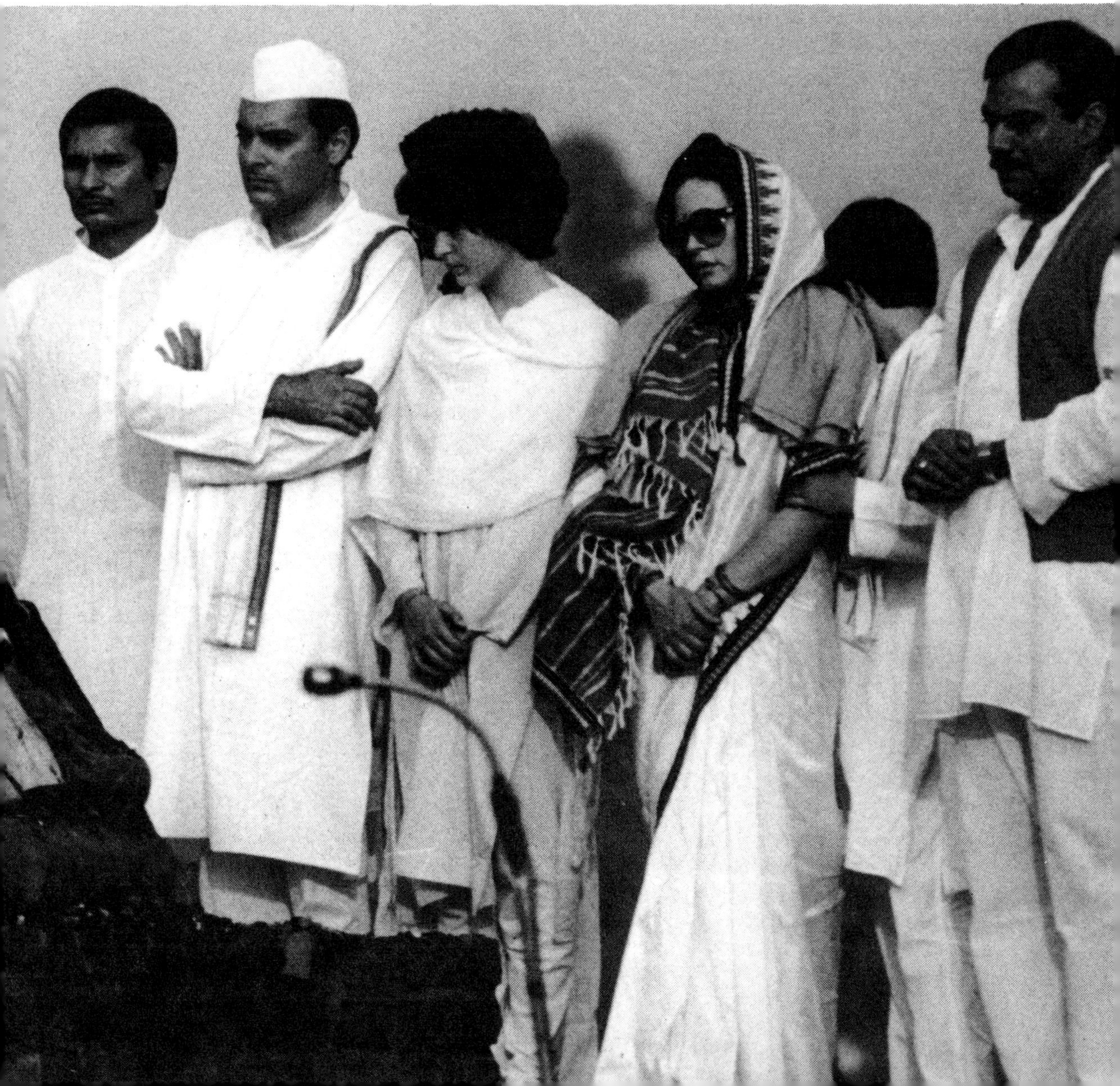

like a tornado. Furious Hindus turned on the Sikh population in a murderous wave of vengeance. Some Hindus tried to protect the beleaguered Sikhs, but thousands of others raged through the streets of Delhi and other cities, slaughtering whole families of Sikhs, burning their homes and shops. Indira had scoffed at the idea of "punishing a whole community"; now her angry people were doing exactly that.

This is a sad day for India, the United States, and people who stand for democracy around the world.

—GEORGE SHULTZ
U.S. secretary of state, on the death of Indira Gandhi

A few hours after his mother's death, Rajiv was sworn in as prime minister of India. (His appointment was confirmed by the electorate the following December.) As prime minister, Rajiv pleaded with his countrymen to stop the violence. He established refugee camps where the terrified Sikhs could find safety from the rampaging mobs, and he ordered the army and the police to restore order. Slowly, anger was replaced with sorrow. India wept for its dead leader.

Although Indira left her country still poor, still overpopulated, still plagued by food shortages and political corruption, she had fought hard for economic progress and social reform. She was unhesitating about taking power into her own hands when it seemed necessary, but she remained, like Mahatma Gandhi and Jawaharlal Nehru before her, a staunch believer in democracy. Following in her father's footsteps, Indira maintained ties with both the Soviet Union and the United States, considerably expanding India's role as an international force and as a major voice of the Third World.

After an extraordinary life, filled with joy and sorrow, triumph and tragedy, Indira Gandhi achieved in death the goal that had seemed most important to her: she had passed Nehru's office to his grandson. Through Rajiv, Indira would live on.

An elderly Sikh mourns Indira's death. The Indian leader's assassination was followed by a national outpouring of grief from Indians of all faiths—and by a frenzy of vengeful fury against Sikhs. Pleading for calm, Rajiv Gandhi, Indira's son and successor, said, "Indira Gandhi is dead. India is living. India's soul is living."

UPI/BETTMANN NEWSPHOTOS

Further Reading

Ali, Tariq. *An Indian Dynasty*. New York: G. P. Putnam's Sons, 1985.

Bhatia, Krishan. *Indira*. New York: Praeger Publishers, 1974.

Carras, Mary C. *Indira Gandhi in the Crucible of Leadership*. Boston: Beacon Press, 1979.

Hutheesing, Krishna Nehru. *Dear to Behold: An Intimate Portrait of Indira Gandhi*. London: Macmillan, 1969.

Lamb, Beatrice Pitney. *The Nehrus of India, Three Generations of Leadership*. New York: Macmillan, 1967.

Masani, Zareer. *A Biography of Indira Gandhi*. New York: Thomas Y. Crowell Company, 1975.

Mehta, Hansu. *The New India*. New York: Viking Press, 1978.

Mohan, Anand. *Indira Gandhi: A Personal and Political Biography*. New York: Meredith Press, 1967.

Moraes, Dom. *Indira Gandhi*. Boston: Little, Brown and Company, 1980.

Watson, Francis. *A Concise History of India*. New York: Charles Scribner's Sons, 1975.

Chronology

Nov. 19, 1917	Born Indira Priyadashini Nehru in Allahabad, India
1926–27	Travels in Europe with parents, Jawaharlal and Kamala
1929	Organizes children's political organization, the "Monkey Brigade"
Feb. 28, 1936	Mother dies of tuberculosis
1941	Returns to India after six years of study and travel abroad
March 26, 1942	Marries Feroze Gandhi
Sept. 1942–June 1943	Imprisoned by British for supporting Indian civil disobedience
Aug. 20, 1944	Birth of son Rajiv
Dec. 14, 1946	Birth of son Sanjay
Aug. 14, 1947	India achieves independence from Britain; Indira's father, Jawaharlal Nehru, becomes the nation's first prime minister
Jan. 30, 1948	Mohandas Gandhi assassinated by Hindu extremist
1959	Indira Gandhi elected president of ruling Indian National Congress
Sept. 8, 1960	Feroze Gandhi dies of a heart attack
Oct. 20, 1962	China invades India, annexes border territory after defeating Indian army
1964	Indira visits the United States and the Soviet Union
May 26, 1964	Nehru dies from stroke
Aug.–Dec. 1965	Indo-Pakistani War; India repels invasion
Jan. 19, 1966	Indira is elected prime minister of India
1971	Reelected prime minister in landslide victory
Dec. 1971	India is drawn into Pakistan's civil war
April 1974	Indira uses drastic measures to break railroad strike
June 12, 1975	Found guilty of electoral fraud; asked to resign
June 26, 1975	Declares state of emergency due to political unrest; arrests thousands of political opponents
March 1977	State of emergency ends; Indira and her Congress party defeated in national elections by Janata party
Nov. 1978	Elected to Parliament; barred from taking her seat and briefly jailed
Jan. 3, 1980	Elected prime minister for the third time
June 23, 1980	Indira's son Sanjay dies in plane crash
June 1981	Indira's son Rajiv wins parliamentary seat
June 6, 1984	Indian army storms the Golden Temple at Amritsar, kills Sikh secessionist leader
Oct. 31, 1984	Indira Gandhi assassinated by Sikh extremists; Rajiv named prime minister

Index

Francelia Butler is Professor of English at the University of Connecticut. A leader in the establishment of children's literature as a major field in the humanities, she is the founder and current editor-in-chief of the scholarly annual, *Children's Literature*. Her writings include *Children's Literature: A Conceptual Approach*, *Sharing Literature with Children*, and *Masterworks of Children's Literature of the Seventeenth Century*. Butler conducted a private interview with Indira Gandhi in June, 1974.

Arthur M. Schlesinger, jr., taught history at Harvard for many years and is currently Albert Schweitzer Professor of the Humanities at City University of New York. He is the author of numerous highly praised works in American history and has twice been awarded the Pulitzer Prize. He served in the White House as special assistant to Presidents Kennedy and Johnson.